Holy Days

A Year of Spiritual Celebration

H.H. Pujya Swami Chidanand Saraswatiji

GANGA
PRESS

Swami Chidanand Saraswati, 2004
Holy Days: A Year of Spiritual Celebration
ISBN: 978-0-9831490-2-6

Please contact us at:
Parmarth Niketan
P.O. Swargashram; Rishikesh (Himalayas); Uttarakhand - 249 304, India
Ph: (0135) 2440011, 2434301; Fax: (0135) 2440066
swamiji@parmarth.com
www.parmarth.com & www.ihrf.com
Note: from abroad, dial + 91-135 instead of (0135) for phone and fax

Illustrations by Rozalia Hummel (Radhikapriya)
Cover art by Dawn Ballie
Typeset by sevaks at Parmarth Niketan Ashram

Acknowledgements

We would like to offer special thanks to the following people for their loving and dedicated *seva* in bringing this book to fruition: H.H. Sri Shankaracharya Swami Divyanand Teerthji read the first draft of the book and offered insightful comments and suggestions. Rozalia Hummel (Radhika Priya), upon hearing about this book, immediately offered to create illustrations for it. Thus, she has helped to create our first illustrated publication. Dawn Baillie, our divine cover artist, who brought beauty and magic to the front and back covers. Anar and Avani Mashruwala who provided invaluable comments – from the perspective of Hindu youth living in the West – on the content of the first draft.

Table of Contents

The Rituals

For More Information

Blessings
H.H. Sri Shankaracharyaji Swami Divyanand Teerthji,
Bhanpura Peeth

Das Kabeer has said, "If you want to get a pearl you have to dive deep into the waters." Similarly, if one wants a diamond, one will have to pierce deeply into a rock. Thus, if someone wants to change society, he needs to deeply know all aspects of life.

Sri Swami Chidanandji Saraswati is a serious, profound thinker who has a deep knowledge of all aspects of life and thus can provide a practical guide to humanity. It is not my habit to praise someone, but the truth has to be expressed. I have always found him to be a saint of great devotion to the Lord and he is a divine light dedicated selflessly to the service of society.

In his present work *Holy Days: A Year of Spiritual Celebration*, Sri Swamiji has emphasized that one should devote one's festivals to the Lord. Surrender unto Him is the key to turning each day of one's life into a pure day – a Holy Day.

I believe that this book will inspire humanity in general and youth in particular to turn their holidays into holy days.

May the Lord give Swami Chidanandji strength to continue to serve the Lord and humanity with such positive, constructive and transformative thoughts, ideas and deeds.

Swami Divyanand Teerth

Introduction

It is Diwali. Everyone is dressed in new, sparkling clothes. Silk and chiffon *sarees* drape elegantly off the shoulders of the women as they mingle, exchanging hugs, gifts, good wishes and compliments on each others' new clothing. Youth – a mix of those whose steadfastness won out against their parents' pleas and are thus adorned in their jeans and t-shirts, and those who enjoy the beauty and elegance of Indian clothing – cling to each other in groups, whispering, giggling, making plans for later that evening. A group of devotees is seated in a semi-circle around the image of Goddess Lakshmi, performing Her *puja*. The priest chants soul-stirring mantras, prayers and *shlokas* as the devotees perform the intricate rites of the Diwali puja. Some ladies, a few of their husbands, and a handful of the youth make their way around the temple and outside up the pathways, gracefully lighting a nearly infinite row of small, delicate oil lamps. They kneel down, one by one, as the small wicks swimming in oil are lit. Soon the temple lights are shut off and the brilliance of the oil lamps fills the room. Brightly flickering flames cast elegant dancing shadows on the walls.

As the *puja* finishes, the lights are switched on and tray after tray of sweets are distributed. Children rush, hands outstretched to receive the *ladoos* and other *prasad*.

A joyous time, full of light, love, and laughter, Diwali is probably the most widely-celebrated Hindu holiday across the world. But why? Why do we celebrate Diwali? Even more significantly, what can we learn from Diwali? Let us ask not only what is its historical and spiritual meaning, but let us also ask, what is its meaning in our lives today?

While every Hindu in every country is sure to light a lamp and distribute sweets on this day, how many of us go to sleep on the night of Diwali a better person than we were when we woke up that morning? How many of us truly contemplate the years Bhagwan Rama lived in the forest and the glory of His return to Ayodhya? How many of us contemplate the nature of good versus evil? How many of us carefully inspect our hearts, our minds, our motivations, and our actions on this day? How many of us think of all that which is dark – in every aspect of our lives – and pray for it to become light?

By the time the sun rises on the morning after Diwali, all of the lamps are extinguished. Our new clothes are no longer new. Our stomachs gurgle from overindulgence in sweets. But has anything changed within us? Is this day any different than the day before? The answer should be 'yes,' but unfortunately it frequently is 'no.'

This picture painted of Diwali could just as easily be Janmasthami or Ram Navami or Guru Purnima, or any one of a variety of sacred holidays celebrated throughout the Hindu year. Hindus celebrate with great devotion and piety, and with a dedication unparalleled by any other religious group I have ever seen. It is common for people to chant 108 *Hanuman Chalisas* during the course of a day, or to perform 1008 *ahutis* in a *yagna* or to spend hours engaged in intricate *puja* ceremonies, offering water, milk, flowers, incense and *aarti* to God as enchanting Vedic mantras are chanted.

However, although they perform this worship with great devotion and piety, many of them admit not knowing the deepest meaning and significance of the rituals or celebrations. This is particularly true in the youth.

One of the great and unique aspects of Pujya Swamiji's teachings is that they always include information about how we can change. His explanations and answers never stop at the mere meaning or external significance of a particular ritual or holiday. Rather, He uses every opportunity to teach us how to better ourselves. It is not uncommon to hear Him say, *"But the real question is how to have Janmashtami [or Diwali or Navratri…] take place inside of you. The real question is how to make your life Janmashtmi [or Diwali or Navratri…]."*

Thus, this book serves two purposes. First, it gives Hindus everywhere the meaning – historical and spiritual – of these major holidays. Hindu youth can share unabashedly with their friends, *"We celebrate Diwali because it marks the day that Lord Rama returned from his exile in the jungle. But it really signifies the victory of light over darkness and of good over evil."* Adults can educate their colleagues, *"We light these* dias *to signify the way God removes darkness from our life with His divine light. This* dia *represents the light of knowledge, the light of compassion and the light of love."*

Second, the book teaches us how these beautiful holidays apply to our lives today and how we can transform ourselves with each and every holiday. Pujya Swamiji infuses the explanation of each holiday with an explanation of how we should use the holiday to become better people.

Hindus across the Western world should proudly (and knowledgably) share with their friends, associates and colleagues the deep, rich meaning of their culture. The youth should not be ashamed of the intricate rituals, nor should they shy away from participating for fear that their friends might not approve. Rather, they should proudly and boldly participate in activities which celebrate not only historical events, but that also truly signify a time for us to replenish ourselves spiritually. Hindu holidays are filled with ways and reasons for us to examine our lives, measure our progress and re-affirm our commitment to follow the path of *dharma*, of righteousness and of integrity.

Through this book, the young, the old, the traditional, the modern, the conservative, the liberal, the Indian and the non-Indian will find the historical, spiritual and mythological significance to the myriad festivals, as well as inspiring, compelling reasons to celebrate. Most importantly, they will learn how to make their holidays true holy days.

Sadhvi Bhagwati
Rishikesh, India, May 2004

The Holidays

Rama Navami

Rama Navami is the day on which Bhagwan Rama, the seventh incarnation of Bhagwan Vishnu, incarnated in human form in the holy land of Ayodhya. It falls on the ninth day of the bright fortnight in the month of Chaitra (March/April). The word *"Rama"* literally means one who is divinely blissful and who gives joy to others, and one in whom the sages rejoice.

It is said that the repetition of His name (*Rama Nama*) is the surest, fastest and easiest way to attain purity, peace, wisdom, understanding, joy, prosperity, and ultimately liberation. Bhagwan Rama Himself said, "Repetition of My name once is equal to the repetition of one thousand names of God or to the repetition of a mantra one thousand times." As the founder of the nation, Mahatma Gandhiji, collapsed to his death after having been viciously shot, he had no words of vengeance or anger for his murderers. Rather, the only words which escaped his lips with his dying breath were, *"He Rama, He Rama, He Rama."*

On the beautiful day that Bhagwan Rama came to Earth, let us ask ourselves the meaning of His life. What lessons did He incarnate to teach the world? What lessons do we learn from the *Ramayana*, the glorious depiction of Bhagwan Rama's life?

Bhagwan Rama exemplified the perfect person; He embodied the divine on Earth, and He taught us how to live our lives in accordance with *dharma* and divine principles. Bhagwan Rama was the embodiment of compassion, gentleness, kindness, righteousness and integrity. Although He had all the power in the world, He was still peaceful and gentle. Through careful examination of His life, we learn how to be the perfect son, the perfect brother, the perfect husband and the perfect king. His reign in Ayodha is referred to as *Ramarajya*, the epitome of perfect governance.

The story of the *Ramayana* is a classic, eternal, universal message of *dharma* versus *adharma*, of *deva* versus demon, of good versus evil, represented in the battle between Rama and Ravana.

Ravana was a *brahmin*; he was a great scholar who wrote numerous works on scriptural philosophy. He was powerful, dynamic, and beautiful in appearance. As the brilliant, handsome king of Lanka, he had everything one would need to be happy and peaceful.

Yet, I have never once heard of any child – anywhere in the world – named Ravana. Why? Why does every mother name her child Rama, and no parents, ever, have thought to name their son Ravana? What made Ravana – this great learned scholar – a demon? What made Rama God and Ravana a demon?

Both were kings; both were learned in the scriptures; both were charismatic; both were beautiful. Yet, there was one main difference: Bhagwan Rama's heart overflowed with divinity, love, generosity, humility, and a sense of duty. Ravana's heart, in contrast, was filled with avarice, hatred, and egoism. Under Bhagwan Rama's divine touch, the animals became His devotees and His divine helpers. Under Ravana's touch, even humans became animals.

Ravana was arrogant, egoistic, greedy and lustful. His insatiable desires led him to crave more and more power, more and more money, and more and more beautiful ladies to fulfill his every whim.

Covetous desires can never be fulfilled, and the cease-less quest for them brings only frustration. Therefore, regardless of how smart we are, how rich we are, or how beautiful we are, we are demons if our hearts are filled with anger and greed. This is, in essence, the difference between Bhagwan Rama and Ravana.

It says *Ravayati iti Ravanah*. This means that anyone who makes people cry is a Ravana. Anyone who brings joy to others is Rama.

Bhagwan Rama was in peace; Ravana was in pieces. So, how can we become like Bhagwan Rama? How to be godly and peaceful and righteous? How to win the war of Lanka within ourselves? Bhagwan Rama has given us the perfect example through His life and His actions. The way to attain divinity, the way to be "perfect," the way to be in peace instead of pieces, is to follow His clear example.

Bhagwan Rama's primary message is: fulfill your duty without any selfish motives; put other people before yourself. When He was exiled to the forest, Bhagwan Rama did not complain, "But that's not fair." He did not fight back in anger. Rather, He helped His father fulfill a promise; He lived according to His duty as a son and as a future king. He did not once think about Himself, His own comforts, or His own "rights." Rather, He abided by His *dharma* and His duty.

The message of the *Ramayana* is:

Choose *Dharma* over *Artha*
Choose *Moksha* over *Kama*

According to Hindu tradition, the four goals of life are *Dharma, Artha, Kama* and *Moksha*. All are important. All are necessary for a full, complete, fulfilling life. *Dharma* is translated loosely as "the right path" or the "path of righteousness." *Artha* is the fulfillment of one's career or professional path. *Kama* is the fulfillment of one's path of physical intimacy (i.e. marriage), and *Moksha* is the attainment of God-realization.

Bhagwan Rama teaches us that when given the choice, *Dharma* must be chosen over *Artha*. When Bhagwan Rama's father, Dashratha, the King of Ayodhya, was compelled to banish Rama to the forest for fourteen years instead of coronating Him as King, Bhagwan Rama took the path of *Dharma* by peacefully and agreeably leaving the kingdom for the forest rather than choosing the path of *Artha*, His duty as the future King of Ayodhya. Then, at the end of the *Ramayana*, Bhagwan Rama shows us to choose *Moksha* over *Kama*. After the war in Lanka, Bhagwan Rama must leave Sitaji in the forest, for his subjects doubt her chastity. How easy it would have been to choose His own happiness over His subjects' faith. How easy it would have been for Him to say, "You are all stupid! You are all just suspicious." But, He did not say that. Bhagwan Rama knew that He was a king first and a husband second. His primary duty was to His kingdom, to bring health, happiness and prosperity to His subjects. Having Sitaji remain in Ayodhya would bring only resentment and disharmony. Therefore, He acted, once again, according to selfless duty and chose his kingdom over His own marital happiness.

Through His noble and divine choices, He taught the world to choose *dharma* over *artha* and to choose *moksha* over *kama*.

Bhagwan Rama teaches us:

As a son: Respectfully and lovingly obey your father's orders. Sacrifice your own comfort for your father's dignity.

As a step-son: Even when your step-mother (or mother-in-law) is not kind to you, even when she clearly discriminates against you in favor of her own birth child, do not resent her, do not fight against her. Respect her and her wishes.

As a brother: Remain loyal to your brother. Care for him.

As a husband: Protect your wife. Fight for her protection and her purity. But there are times when one's divine path must even take precedence over the path of householder. Do not keep the role of householder as the ultimate role.

As a King: Sacrifice everything for your people. Do not worry about your own comfort, your own convenience or your own pleasure. Be willing to put the Kingdom ahead of your own needs.

Ravana's ego led to his own demise – first the demise of his spirit and heart, then the demise of his body. He thought he was the one who ran everything. He thought that he was the "doer" of it all. On the other hand, Bhagwan Rama was always humble, and He never took credit for anything. At the end of the war in Lanka, Bhagwan Rama was giving Sitaji a tour of the city, showing her where all of the various events had occurred. When they reached the place where Bhagwan Rama victoriously slew Ravana, He reported it to Sitaji only as, "This is where Ravana died." He didn't say, "This is where I crushed the demon," or ,"This is where I killed Ravana." No. Even after achieving this great victory, He simply stated, "This is where Ravana died."

As we celebrate this holiday, as we revel in Bhagwan Rama's appearance, let us ask ourselves, "Is Rama living inside us? Has the good in our hearts taken birth? Has the power of *dharma* vanquished the power of *adharma* within us?"

Ram Navami is not only a holiday about Bhagwan Rama. It is a holy day about examining ourselves. Life is so short. We never know when the end will come. Do we want to let Ravana live in us? Do we want to be controlled by Ravana? We must give birth today to the Divine in our own hearts. We must let Bhagwan Rama live in our own hearts. We must make a pledge on this day to let purity, honesty, humility and righteousness be the guiding factors in our lives.

Hanuman Jayanti

Hanuman Jayanti is celebrated on the full moon day (*Purnima*) of the month of Chaitra Shukla (March – April). The day commemorates the life of Sri Hanuman, a divine incarnation who embodies the perfect devotee. Hanumanji was the son of the God of wind.

In the Heavenly, Divine Realms, there was a girl named Punjik-asthala who was an attendant to Brihaspati, the preceptor of the gods. However, one time she insulted a sage, and thus she was cursed to be born on Earth as a female monkey, a curse which could only be removed by giving birth to a son who would be an incarnation of Lord Shiva.

Thus, she took birth as Anjana and later married Kesari. Both were very pious and pure, and they lived a life filled with austerities, worship, meditation and penance. Anjana prayed to the God of Wind, Vayu that He would grace her with a son. He fulfilled this wish and graced her with Hanumanji. She also prayed to Lord Shiva to take birth in her womb, thereby freeing her from the curse of living as a female monkey. Lord Shiva was pleased by her purity and devotion and also by her intense spiritual practice; therefore, He agreed to incarnate in her womb as her son.

In that way, the divine Hanumanji took birth on the 14th day of the month of Chaitra in a cave on the Rushyamuk mountain. Upon his birth, Anjana was freed from the curse and able to return to the Heavenly realms. She told Hanuman that the world would provide him fruit as bright and ripe as the rising sun. Mistaking the actual sun for fruit to eat, Hanumanji flew toward the Sun and was just about to swallow it when Indra threw his vajra ("thunderbolt") at Hanumanji to prevent him doing so. The vajra injured Hanumanji and he fell to the Earth.

Vayu, the God of Wind and Hanumanji's divine father, became furious that Indra had injured his son. Out of anger, Vayu stopped the wind from blowing, and all became still. Without the flow of fresh air, life on Earth and also in the Heavenly abode became endangered. Thus, all of the gods went to Vayu to try to appease his anger and to convince him to allow the wind to flow again. In order to placate Vayu, the gods bestowed numerous boons and powers upon Hanuman, including invincibility and fearlessness.

The life of Lord Hanuman is filled with feats of courage and displays of immeasurable strength.

However, what makes Hanumanji so special and divine is not his invincible strength or fortitude, but rather his unwavering and boundless devotion to Lord Rama. From the moment Hanumanji first had Lord Rama's *darshan*, he dedicated his life only to the service of Lord Rama.

Today, in every temple of Bhagwan Rama and Sitaji, there is always a Hanumanji *murti* as well. The true devotee is inseparable from the object of devotion.

Hanumanji demonstrated the omnipotent power of faith

and devotion. He was able to fly across the ocean, to become the size of a giant and also the size of a tiny creature, simply by chanting the name of Lord Rama. When he was sent to bring four precious life-saving herbs from the Himalayas in order to save Lakshman's life, instead of bringing only the four plants, he carried the entire Himalayan mountain! When everyone marveled at the feats he achieved, he simply said, "I am a servant of Lord Rama and I have simply taken His divine name."

Sometimes in life when we embark upon a new, noble undertaking we may be faced with obstacles and hurdles. However, we must always remember that faith and devotion to God are the greatest sources of power. Through chanting God's name with true devotion, we can achieve anything. The power of God's name gave Hanumanji the ability to fly across the ocean and to carry mountains. We must have faith that that power will also work for us.

Yet, the key was Hanumanji's fervent, ardent, single-minded *shraddha* (faith) in God and his tenacious dedication to fulfilling whatever *seva* he could do for God. With such deep, true devotion and dedication, nothing could stop him.

Hanumanji wanted nothing in exchange for his service to Lord Rama. He, as the epitome of selfless devotion, wanted only to have Lord Rama's presence in his life at all times.

One day, Sitaji presented Hanumanji with a garland of pearls as a gift for his valour, Hanumanji was not pleased with this

---

expensive gift. He took the string of pearls and began to break each pearl in half, one by one. "What are you doing?" onlookers exclaimed, as he destroyed the expensive garland. "I am looking for Lord Rama. If this is really a gift for me, then Lord Rama must be here in these pearls. Otherwise they are worthless."

On this day of Hanuman Jayanti, let us strive to be as single-minded in our devotion as Hanumanji. Let us pray that our hearts and even our blood may be filled only with the *raas* ("divine essence") of God and our Guru. Let us sing the glories of such pure devotion and let us seek to emulate Hanumanji's boundless fidelity.

Buddha Jayanti

The Buddha was born on the full-moon day (*Purnima*) in the month of Vaisakh (May) in 563 BC. It is said that he also achieved Enlightenment and attained *Mahasamadhi* (departed the Earthly realm) on the same date.

There are so many beautiful lessons to learn from the life of the Buddha. His life is the epitome of Enlightenment in action.

The word *Buddha* literally means "The Enlightened One" or "The Awakened One." The Buddha was born as Siddhartha Gautama in the 5th century B.C. in the region of Sakyam near the Himalayas. Today, that area lies in Nepal at Lumbini. Siddhartha was born to a father who was most probably a King.

Legend has it that when he was born, an astrologer told Siddhartha's father that his son would either be an emperor or a sanyasi (holy renunciant). His father understood that in order to prevent his son from renouncing the material world in favor of the spiritual world, he would have to keep him sheltered and protected. Thus, Siddhartha was raised in the castle, in the utmost of luxury and comfort and may never even have been allowed a view of the outside world.

At the tender age of sixteen, perhaps to avert the prophecy of him taking to a life of spirituality, Siddhartha was married to Yasodhara and they lived a protected, regal life.

Legend says that finally, after a childhood of being sheltered and protected from the harsh realities of the world, he one day told the charioteer to take him to the city. Along the way, he saw a sick man. The charioteer explained the meaning of illness, for Siddhartha had never before seen or heard of anyone who was not in the peak of health. "Everyone gets sick sometimes," the charioteer explained to the bewildered Siddhartha.

Later, Siddhartha saw an old man walking with a cane along the side of the road. "Why is he walking like that? Why is his hair so white and his step so slow? Is he also sick?" Siddhartha asked. The charioteer explained to Siddhartha that the man was simply old and that everyone eventually becomes old. "Everyone?" Siddhartha inquired incredulously. "Yes, everyone," the charioteer confirmed.

As they drove through the city, Siddhartha saw four men carrying a casket in a funeral procession to the crematorium. "What are they doing?" Siddhartha asked his charioteer. As the charioteer explained about death, Siddhartha was stunned, and immediately realized the inevitably transitory nature of our time on Earth. His mind was deeply troubled however about the sufferings that life brings.

On the way back to the castle, Siddhartha saw a man dressed in orange robes sitting peacefully under a tree, eyes closed in meditation. "Who is that?" Siddhartha asked his charioteer. "That is an ascetic," said the charioteer, "a man who has devoted himself to find the true meaning of life beyond all suffering."

Upon returning to the castle, filled with the knowledge of sickness, old age and death, but having realized that there was a way out of this cycle, Siddhartha renounced the material world for the search of Truth. "If sickness, old age and death are inevitable on this path of life, then surely the nature of existence and the point of life must be deeper than what we are currently experiencing," he thought. With that, he left the castle to spend many years in sadhana *deep in the forest.*

One glimpse of sickness, age and death, and the Buddha realized the temporary and elusive nature of material existence is. We, however, get sick over and over again. We watch our loved ones age, and we have seen so many deaths. However, we never seem to get the message. We continue to run after transitory pleasure and material wealth with the illusion that somehow these are the point of our existence on Earth. We see so many wealthy people and accomplished businessmen pass out of this body empty-handed, yet we continue to run after wealth. This is the nature of our ignorance. The Buddha had one glimpse of sickness and death, and he saw the truth. We must also try to see this truth, for we have not only glimpsed evidence of the ephemeral nature of life but we also live it and experience it daily.

The Buddha went to the forest to seek enlightenment and to find the Truth. Thus, people ask, "So, must we also leave everything to see the Truth." No. Once Edison discovered the laws of electricity, we merely have to use these laws and apply them in our daily lives. We do not have to rediscover them. Once Newton developed the laws of physics, we use these laws in our lives and in our work. We do not have to rediscover these laws. We only need to use them and apply them.

Similarly, the Buddha went to the forest and discovered the Truth. We don't have to leave everything, go to the forest and rediscover this. We only have to take the Truth that he discovered and apply it in our lives.

It is said that first Siddhartha went to study with several spiritual leaders of the time. However, after mastering their teachings he still found that he had not attained the enlightened state. Therefore, he turned his attention to severe austerities, hoping to reach enlightenment through ardent penance and tapasya. Yet, this path also did not bear the fruit he wished and thus he turned to what he would later call the "middle" path, a path which includes teachings and sadhana but is balanced and not severe.

On the full moon day of Vaisakh (April – May), on the banks of the Nerañjara river, he sat beneath a pipal tree, which is regarded as one of the "holy" trees in the Hindu scriptures. This tree would later be known as the "Bodhi tree" in honor of the Buddha's enlightenment in its shade. As he sat, he vowed that he would not stand up until he had attained his goal. Throughout the night he sat, and as the sun rose young Siddhartha (it is said he was thirty-five at the time) had become the Buddha, the "Enlightened One."

However, once he attained this state, what did he do? Did he stay in the forest and continue only to enjoy the divine ecstasy of union with God? Did he spend all of his time in meditation, *puja* and silence? No. After a few short weeks reveling in the bliss of divine union, he came back to the world and started serving. He immediately started to share this treasure chest of wisdom with all. Whatever he knew, whatever he had realized, he spent every minute of his life sharing with everyone who would listen.

The Buddha developed a system, which is now known as Buddhism, that involves four basic principles: 1) Suffering is an inherent component of life; 2) The root of our suffering lies in our desires; 3) By removing our desires and attachments, we can be free of suffering; and 4) The suffering can be ended.

Through the Eight-Fold Path, the Buddha laid out a simple yet clear system for peace, equanimity and ultimately enlightenment.

The Buddha's gift was his wisdom. So, he spent his life traveling from village to village, sharing this knowledge with all. Our gifts may be different. Our gifts may be certain talents or may be our financial wealth or may be something else. But, we must take this message to heart. We all must spend our lives sharing our gifts with the world. Whatever gifts God has bestowed upon us – whether divine knowledge, expertise in a certain field, a particular talent, or financial wealth – we must share them with all.

He not only preached the Truth, but he lived the Truth

One day, as the Buddha was traveling on foot preaching his divine knowledge, a local man spat on him and verbally abused him. And what did the Buddha do? He remained very quiet and very still while the man continued his abusive tirade. At the end, he asked the man "Aur kooch kehana hai?" ("Do you have anything else to say?")

The following day, when the Buddha was again passing through the same place, the man came up to him, fell at his feet and begged forgiveness. He said, "All night long I could not sleep for the abuses I hurled at Your Holiness. Please forgive me." The Buddha replied, "Forgive whom? For what? You are not the same person as the one who abused me yesterday. You have realized and changed. So, whom should I forgive? The 'you' of today needs no forgiving and the 'you' of yesterday is no longer with us. That which happened is like water in a river. It is long since gone, and the river is still flowing."

This is the Buddha's message: Be calm and move on. Do not react.

The Buddha represents fullness. He was born on a full moon. He attained enlightenment on a full moon. He departed this body on a full moon. When we are full inside, then nothing outside can affect us. When we are full inside, then we become unrockable and unshockable. We become shock-proof and rock-proof. It is only when we are empty inside that we react to little things in the outside world.

The true test of spirituality, the true test of "fullness" is not how nicely and peacefully you can sit in meditation on a deserted mountain. Rather, the true test of spirituality is how calmly and peacefully you can live in the world without being affected by the world. The real test of "fullness" is how you can be unshockable and unrockable by the ups and downs of the world.

We spend so much energy to earn money so that we can have expensive air conditioning in our homes and in our cars. But, inside of us, the heat is still on. Our hearts and our minds ignite in flames at the slightest insult or disappointment or failure. We must learn to be cool on the inside. We must learn to have the A/C on inside!

Be calm and move on. Let us take this as our mantra on this day of Buddha Purnima. Let us be filled with spirituality, with God, with love and with piety so that there is no room for us to be affected by little things.

Let us realize the true, temporary and illusory nature of the material world, and instead dedicate ourselves to Truth, to God, and to spirituality. Let us give, give and give whatever we have to others. This is the message of the Buddha.

Guru Purnima

Guru Purnima is celebrated on the full moon day of Ashadha (July-August), at the beginning of the four month period of Chaturmas (the holy time of year in which the monsoons come and the saints refrain from movement). It is the day in which we offer our thanks, love and devotion to the Guru. The *Guru Gita* says "The Guru is Brahma, Vishnu, and Shiva. Verily, the Guru is the Supreme Brahman itself."

But what is a *"guru"* in practical terms? While in the West, the term has taken on myriad, frequently derogatory connotations, the true meaning is pure and simple. In Sanskrit, *"gu"* means darkness, and *"ru"* means one who removes. So, a *"guru"* is one who removes our darkness. It is one whose mere presence emanates so much light, so much love and so much divinity that every darkness within us is alchemically changed into light. There is no darkness too dark for a guru. Their light can shine through and transform even the darkest darkness. Even the darkness of midnight would last but a second if the sun decided to rise six hours early. Similarly, no darkness can last in the Divine presence of a true guru.

Unlike a "preacher" or "minister" or "rabbi," a guru does not necessarily have to be a religious figure, nor does it have to be a person of a specific religion, gender, age or ethnicity. It is simply someone who holds the light for you if your path becomes shrouded in darkness; it is someone who will carry you if you get tired; it is someone who – after you have been in his or her presence – you are not the same. You are lighter, freer, and more filled with joy. It is someone in whose light you want to bask forever.

In the West, guru is frequently defined as "teacher." Yet, the crucial difference between a teacher and a guru is that while teachers can explain concepts and give you verbal information, they cannot actually take you to the realms of which they teach. An astronomy teacher can tell you about other planets, but cannot take you there. A science teacher can explain life on the bottom of the ocean, but cannot take you there. A geology teacher can explain the properties of diamonds to you, but he cannot fill your hands with the precious gems. In contrast, a guru not only teaches you about God, but rather, he takes you to God. He not only teaches you about peace, but he also gives you peace.

In Sanskrit, the word "guru" means one who removes our darkness. Yet it is not merely the darkness of ignorance. It is not simply that we go to our guru with a question, ask him, receive an answer and our confusion clears. Rather, the mere presence of the guru in our life removes all darkness – all anger, all pain, all confusion.

History of Guru Purnima

Guru Purnima is the day on which we pay our reverence

to the Guru. It is a day filled with devotion, love and piety. On this day, Indians across the world pay their deepest reverence to both their personal guru, as well as to Sri Maharishi Vyasji. Vyasji is heralded as the one who classified and arranged the four Vedas, and as the author of the eighteen *Puranas*, the *Mahabharata* and the *Bhagavad Gita*. Having brought such an immeasurable treasure chest of wisdom to the world, Vyasji is worshipped as the Great Guru. It is he who brought forth this ocean of divine light to dispel the darkness of humanity. Therefore, on this day we also pay our deepest respects to Sri Vyasji.

The Guru Quenches Our Thirst

In India, the summer is followed by the monsoon season when the skies themselves seem to open, pouring down sheets of water upon the parched land. After the long, hot, dry months of summer in which innumerable people, animals and crops may have perished, the rains finally come, quenching our thirst and bringing us life. And in India, when the rains come, it is not a mere drizzle. Rather, the rains are downpours of heavenly nectar, completely saturating the dry land.

Similarly, on this day of Guru Purnima as we find ourselves dying of thirst for knowledge, understanding and peace, as we find our hearts and minds have become dry due to ignorance, anger and darkness, the Guru comes, pouring forth upon our lives the rain of wisdom, love, light and life. Just as the flowers which have wilted and yellowed in the never-ending heat of summer suddenly stand erect and succulent as soon as the rains come, so we, who have become ignorant and "dead" to the divinity within us, are immediately born anew due to His grace in our lives.

The monsoon comes only once a year. The ground and soil are graced only one season a year with the divine flow of rain. However, the Guru is always with us. His grace is always showering upon us. There is only one "monsoon season," but if we allow the Guru's grace into our lives, then every season is the season of the Guru.

Yet, just as the soil must allow the rain to penetrate its depths in order to reap the benefits of this life-giving nectar, so we must become porous vessels into which the divine nectar of the Guru can flow.

The most important quality in a disciple is humility and surrender to the Guru. If we are filled with our own ego, then there is no room for the Guru's grace to flow.

There is a story of a man who had done many years of scriptural study but he hadn't attained the height of spiritual progress which he was craving. He had heard that there was an enlightened master who lived on a mountain in the Himalayas. So, he traveled the great distance to find this master.

When he finally reached the Guru's cave in the mountains, he was filled with excitement at being so close to attaining what he had always wanted. When he beheld the Master, he bowed at the Master's feet and started to tell the Master everything he had studied, practiced and learned. He explained where he felt that he was stuck on his spiritual path, and all of the obstacles he faced. The Master was quiet. When the man finished talking, the Master calmly said, "Let us have a cup of tea."

"Tea?!" the seeker exclaimed. "But Gurudev, I have travelled weeks on foot to find you. I have spent years and years in the quest for enlightenment. I am now at Your holy feet waiting for You to bestow Your great wisdom upon me. I don't want tea! Just bless me with Divine Liberation."

"First we will have tea," the Master said calmly, and laid out two cups for tea. The Guru then began to pour tea from a kettle into each cup. As he filled the seeker's cup, the man watched as the Guru poured and poured even though the tea reached to the rim of the cup. Then, still, as the cup overflowed and tea spilled onto the floor, the Guru kept pouring.

"Gurudev," the man said. "Stop. It is enough. Can you not see that the tea is now spilling out on the floor? There is no more room in the cup."

The Guru smiled and stopped pouring. "You are like this cup, my child. Just as the cup is so full that it can hold no more tea, so you are so full of your own ego, your own learning, your own stories, your own explanations, that there is no room for anything else. You cannot hold what I can teach you. Until you empty yourself of your ego, your preconceived ideas, your own book knowledge and your own explanations of how everything is there will be no point in me teaching you at all. You cannot hold anything right now. There is no room."

Similarly, if we really want the grace of the Guru to flow into us and transform our lives, we must become empty vessels. Only when we are empty of ego can He fill us with His divine light.

Faith

Guru Purnima is a day of renewing our faith, our *shraddha*, in He who bestows the light upon our lives. It is a day of re-opening our hearts, our souls and our lives to His divine presence and letting it penetrate and saturate every aspect of our being.

There is a beautiful story told about a man who wanted to walk on water. He begged his guru to give him a secret mantra or a special boon so he could complete this remarkable feat. The man was extremely pious and devoted, and he had been in his guru's service for many years. Therefore, the guru gave him a leaf, folded many times until it was very small. He told his disciple, "Within this leaf is a secret formula which will enable you to walk on water. However, you must not open it because the formula inside is a secret."

So the man agreed, and he took the folded leaf carefully in his hands and began his journey across the river. He was walking successfully on the water when suddenly he was overcome by curiosity and doubt. What could be this secret formula? Is there really a secret inside? Is it a powder or a stone or some holy mantra printed? Where did his guru get it? His doubts got the best of him and he began slowly to open the leaf as he walked, careful lest any of the secret formula should spill out into the water. As soon as he unfolded the last piece to unveil the secret, he suddenly sank into the water and drowned. Inside the leaf was written the simple word, "Faith."

It was not the leaf, nor any secret powder or mantra that enabled the devotee to accomplish a miracle. It was the strength of his faith in his guru and in the "boon" his guru had given him. As soon as that faith wavered and doubt crept in, his life was lost. This is the power of faith.

At this time of Guru Purnima, we must look at what really makes up the Guru-Disciple relationship – what makes it so special, so unique, so powerful and life-transforming?

The key is faith. Faith can work true miracles, and without it much of life is futile. The guru might be of infinite power, knowledge and compassion. Yet, without the faith of the disciple, the guru can do very little for him. There is a beautiful poem that says:

> As children bring their broken toys
> with tears for us to mend,
> I brought my broken dreams to God,
> because He was my friend.
> But, instead of leaving Him in peace to work alone,
> I hung around and tried to help
> with ways that were my own.
> At last I snatched them back and cried,
> "How could you be so slow?"
> "My child," He answered,
> "What could I do? You never did let go."

That "letting go" is faith. If we can surrender to the guru with complete faith, he will transform our lives. However, if we "hang around" and doubt and think that we know better than he does, then we gain nothing.

Choosing a Guru

A guru should not be chosen haphazardly. Most people say that they "just knew" as soon as they met their guru. That is the way it should be. Our hearts should fill with joy in his presence. Our entire beings should feel like they are bathed in warm sunlight. We should instinctively know that he can take us where we need to go.

So, in the early stages, before we take a mantra or before we officially make someone our guru, that is the time to watch and reflect: "Is he (or she) really the one?" However, once we know deep in our hearts and souls that the decision is right, then we should not look back. We should offer ourselves with full abandon at the feet of the guru, and our lives will become magic.

Many people today, especially in the West, are hesitant about what they see as "blind obedience" to the Guru. They feel that somehow they will be lesser people if they become obedient to a master. They don't want to feel like "slaves." I hear this so frequently by people who have been over-indoctrinated by the Western ideal of individuality. Yet, we must realize that we are living our lives as slaves of our own egos and vanity. We live in blind obedience to the call of our senses and desires. We have blind faith in that which our minds and hearts tell us and we act accordingly. But, these false "masters" so frequently lead us astray. We act out of impulse, emotion or vanity and later regret it.

Let us realize that we are, as it is, acting in obedience to a master. Therefore, let us choose a master who will lead us to the light, not the darkness; a master who will lead us to wisdom, not ignorance; a master who will lead us to peace instead of pieces; and a master who will never give us an order we will later regret. Let us live our lives in obedience to the divine orders of our guru instead of in slavery to the volatile callings of our egos, desires and senses.

It is through the teachings of the Guru and through the grace of the Guru that we become masters of our minds, thoughts and senses. Only then can we truly be free.

The *Guru Gita* tells us: "Meditate with concentration upon the Guru's form. Worship with devotion the Guru's feet. Take the Guru's teachings as sacred, perfect mantras and recite them diligently. Only through the Guru's grace will you attain liberation."

The Qualities of a Disciple

People sometimes make the mistake of putting all of the responsibility on the Guru. We expect that we can continue to live our lives exactly as we want – along with our own egos, greed and vices – and yet the Guru will come, wave a magic wand and grant us instant peace, prosperity and enlightenment. It is not like that. The disciple must be dedicated, committed, faithful and assiduous in his/her *sadhana*. A good disciple:

1. Always tells the truth to the Guru and never hides anything from the Guru.

2. Practices the teachings of the Guru with faith, discipline and regularity.

3. Follows the instructions of the Guru without argument. Questions, of course, can and should be asked when there are doubts or confusion in the disciple's mind, but prior to asking any question the disciple should first deeply introspect to see whether the question really warrants the time and attention of the Guru or whether the question is simply to satisfy the ego or desires of the disciple.

4. Continues to grow and develop each day, making a commitment each morning to be more pure, more holy, and more divine every day.

5. Vows to live as a beautiful example and representative of the Guru. Disciples are the reflection of the Guru. So, if we truly love, revere and adore our Gurus, we must pledge to live our lives as shining examples of their teachings and as pure reflections of their Divine lives.

6. Is humble in front of the Guru, accepting the Guru's words (and sometimes reprimands) with surrender and humility.

7. Is ever ready to serve the Guru – any time of the day, any day of the week, any week of the year. *Seva* given by the Guru and performed for the guru is a rare and precious jewel on the road to God-realization. In fact, selfless, dedicated *seva* for the Guru is one of the straightest and clearest paths to ultimate *moksha*.

We must never give up an opportunity to perform *seva* for our Gurus.

The Guru of Nature

Another beautiful aspect of Guru Purnima is represented by the teaching of Dattatreya, who himself is regarded as a Guru of Gurus, and even as an incarnation of God Himself. Dattatreya said that he had twenty-four Gurus, all manifestations of nature. From each of nature's creations, he learned a different lesson, ranging from the selfless service of the fruit-bearing tree to the persistence of the rain drops.

On this day, let us too look around at God's natural creation and ask what we can learn from Mother Nature. Rather than looking upon Her as a commodity to be used and abused, let us look upon Her as a Guru from whom we receive countless lessons and blessings.

August 15th – India's Independence Day

It is the special time of year in which we celebrate the anniversary of Mother India's Independence. We revel in memories of Her strong yet non-violent victory over the British. We shout with pride, *"Bharat Mata ki Jai!"* This ardent pride in our culture and loyalty to our Mother Land and Mother tradition are hallmarks of the Indian people. Many historians have noted that India is the only country where people were colonized so forcibly for so many thousands of years, yet where people lost neither the depth nor richness of their ancient culture, nor did the people's loyalty to their original culture wane or dissipate.

As we celebrate this glorious holiday, as we rejoice in our hard-earned freedom, let us look beyond our external freedom to rule independently. Let us look at whether, internally, the people of India are truly free. *Swarajya* means "self-rule;" it means that we, the Indian people, have control over our own land, our own government and our own rules. So, we achieved outer *swarajya*; we achieved freedom from the British. But, have we achieved inner *swarajya*? Do we, each of us, have control over ourselves? Are we truly free internally?

The chains used to be imposed by the British. They were

overt and obvious. Many of us are still bound by chains, yet these chains are more subtle and insidious. They are the chains of our attachments to worldly possessions; they are the chains of our craving to be more and more Western, thereby leading us to forsake the richness of our culture; they are the chains of corruption – both external and internal; they are the chains of desires for sensual fulfillment.

The chains of our attachments to worldly possessions and sensual pleasures keep us prisoners even more than the British imperial rule. When our focus in life is on attaining more wealth, more material objects, more prestige and fame, and more comforts, then we must live within a set of rules even more limited than those imposed by the colonizers. We must forsake our family for our job. We must spend less time engaged in spiritual pursuits in order to "get ahead" at work. We must travel extensively, thereby weakening the bonds of family. But, most importantly, when we are focused on material success or sensual pleasures, we are not even free in our own minds. Check yourself. Sit quietly. What comes to you first? Is it God? Is it a passage from the scriptures? Is it a desire to go to temple? Or is it a thought about work, a project, or some material object you've been craving to attain? When we are committed primarily to material prosperity, our predominant thoughts tend to be those pertaining to our careers, our investments, our colleagues, our projects and our desires. These concerns trap us and prevent us from finding true freedom in life.

It is wonderful to be successful. It is wonderful to be

prosperous. It is wonderful to be comfortable and to enjoy life. Even in our scriptures, Bhagwan Shri Krishna was a king who lived in a city of gold. However, it is the pre-occupation with the accumulation of more and more that binds us. It is the obsession with "success at all costs" that becomes our captor. In order to be truly free, we must loosen the chains of this attachment. We must perform our duties for God and take whatever comes as *prasad*. We should never become slaves to our desires for possessions, because these desires can never be satiated, and they simply lead to our misery and bondage.

Another chain that, sadly, is enslaving many Indians to-day is the desire to be Western. The Western media – tele-vision, movies, commercials, magazines – have convinced the Indian people, especially our youth, that the keys to happiness lie in being as Western as possible. Thus, they chase after Western fashions, Western entertainment and Western lifestyles. Although the West has a great deal to offer in terms of academic and professional excellence, the materialistic culture does *not* hold the keys to true peace, meaning and joy in life. These keys lie in the ancient, yet timeless, culture of India which emphasizes simplicity, piety and focus on spirituality. They lie in the wisdom of our scriptures. They lie in our rich tradition. Thus, our youth (and now, unfortunately their parents as well) are trapped in a vicious cycle in which, with each effort to become more and more Western, they must forsake another piece of their Indian culture. Although they are searching for deep and lasting happiness, they find only superficial, temporary pleasure.

The key to breaking this chain lies in love and acceptance of Bharat Mata and Her culture. It lies in learning as much as we can – academically, professionally, technically, and scientifically – from the West without abandoning our loyalty to our own value system and our own *sanskaras*. When our children can look at themselves and their friends and say, "I am proud to be Indian," then and only then will they truly be free.

Sadly, we are also bound by chains of corruption within our own hearts. Are we honest people? Are we righteous? Do we uphold the principles of *dharma*? We fought a long, arduous battle to win our right to freedom from the British. Let us truly bask in this freedom, realizing the real richness of our values, ethics and *sanskaras*. The principles set forth in our scriptures are just as applicable to people living in modern Mumbai or Delhi as they were to people living thousands of years ago in the Himalayas. Let us not be bound by the chains of jealousy, anger and greed. These chains bind not only our hands but also our hearts. Instead, let us live lives of generosity, *seva*, love, purity and divinity.

Our country won independence more than fifty years ago. When will we win independence over ourselves? When will we be the ones to determine the path of our lives, rather than let that path be dictated by our desires, our attachments, our lust and our greed? God has given each one of us the veto power. We must exercise it. We are not lightbulbs that can be switched on and off at the will of others. Yet, too frequently, we act like that. Too frequently, we let the rest of the world determine our state of mind, our choices and our values. Let us take our lives back into our own hands, and turn the reins over only to God. When our lives become surrendered to His service, to service for Bharat Mata and to service for *dharma*, then we will be a truly free nation and people.

Krishna Janmasthami

Krishna Janmasthami is the celebration of the day that Bhagwan Krishna incarnated in human form upon the Earth. It is celebrated at midnight on the eighth day of the dark fortnight in the month of Bhadrapada (August-September).

The day is celebrated by worshipping Bhagwan Krishna, fasting and chanting devotional *kirtan* and *bhajans* until past midnight.

The *Bhagavad Gita* says that whenever there is darkness in the world, whenever strife and ignorance prevail, the Lord incarnates to shine His divine light on the darkness. He grabs hold of the faltering world, preventing it from drifting too far astray.

However, the Lord does not simply incarnate, give wisdom and depart. Rather, His divine light, His divine message and His divine grace continue to shine on and on upon all future generations. His wisdom is such that, once given, it is timeless and eternal, infinite and universal. Lord Krishna's message in the *Bhagavad Gita* and the message of His entire life are not meant merely for those who lived 5000 years ago in the lands of Mathura, Vrindavan, Kurukshetra and Dwarka. Rather, the messages are as timeless as His presence and grace.

As we celebrate the divine anniversary of the date He came forth into this world in human form, we must ask ourselves, "Why did He incarnate?" What was the message of Lord Krishna's life? What darkness did He come to dispel? In what ocean of ignorance were we drowning, from which He came to save us?

Most Indians, and now many Westerners as well, are familiar with the *Bhagavad Gita*. We know that Lord Krishna's verbal message to Arjuna on the battlefield was, "Stand up. Do your duty."

However, there are also invaluable lessons and divine teachings embedded in the very life He lived, not only in His 700-verse "Song of God." What are these messages of Bhagwan Krishna's life, and how do they apply to us today? Let us look at His life for these hidden treasures.

Messages from the Incarnation of Lord Krishna

Bhagwan Krishna came to Earth in the darkness of night, into the locked confines of a jail cell where His mother and father were being held prisoners due to His evil uncle Kamsa. However, at the moment of His appearance (in the form of a human infant), all the guards fell asleep, the chains were broken, and the barred doors gently opened. Thus, Vasudeva (Krishna's father) safely and easily carried baby Krishna across the flowing Yamuna to Gokula.

There is a beautiful message here, even from the first moment of the Lord's life. We may be living in the darkness of midnight; we may be bound and chained by so many attachments, temptations, anger, grudges, pains, and by the binding force of *maya*. We may feel ourselves locked into the prison of our own bodies, the prison of duality. However, as soon as we let the Lord live in our own hearts, all darkness fades, all chains are broken and all prison doors open freely. Wherever the Lord is, there are no locks.

Also, we can see that the door to the Lord – from any direction, inside or outside – is always open. The only lock is the lock of our own ignorance and our own illusions. As soon as that ignorance is dispelled, as soon as we see His glowing form, all the doors in this life and in all lives open to us.

The Childhood of the Lord

Beginning with His appearance in a jail and the immediate rush to whisk Him away to a new family, across Yamunaji in Gokula, the Lord was not given an "easy" childhood.

On the sixth day of the Lord's life, Putna (the demoness) made Him drink poison from her breast. In His third month of life a bullock cart collapsed on Him. Then, when He was four, huge trees fell on Him.

Until the age of eleven, He was in Vrindavan and Govardhan. The people of Govardhan worshipped Indra, singing his praises and making daily offerings to him. However, Bhagwan Krishna admonished them and said that they should worship Govardhan instead, since it was Govardhan who gave them land, water, and grass for their cows. Yet, the people were afraid. Indra threatened to wreak havoc upon their lives if they ceased his worship. As Indra pummeled the beautiful land of Govardhan with rain, hail, thunder and lightening, the Lord held up the mountain of Govardhan over the heads of the people, protecting them from the violent storm. However, as He held up this mountain on the tip of His finger, for days and days as Indra grew more and more furious, He never became angry, nor frustrated, nor disheartened. He was always smiling, even in the midst of the torrential storm.

A few short years later, He was forced to kill His uncle and had to flee His home in Mathura, barefoot to Junagar, with nothing but a small pitambar. For years then, this King of all Kings lived in a simple ashram, doing seva for the saints with no facilities, no amenities and no comfort. He had no coat for winter, no umbrella for the rains...

Yet, wherever Bhagwan Krishna went, wherever He was, He was always blissful, always joyful, always shining His divine light upon others.

We, on the other hand, may get stuck in one traffic jam and our days are ruined. We have one business failure and we feel dejected and broken. We become afflicted with disease and we lose our faith in God.

The Message of His Life

So, what is the Lord teaching us? If He chose His birth and He chose the course of His life on Earth, why did He choose a life full of obstacles, turmoil, trials and tribulations? Why, if He could have lived His entire life as a king, did He spend so many years living in the jungle?

He did this to show us that the real palace is the palace of our heart. When our hearts are full of God, then we live constantly in the most beautiful Golden Palace, regardless of where our bodies may be. He chose this life to teach us that regardless of what insults are hurled at us or what obstacles we face, we must remain immersed in Divine Connection. Then we will not become depressed or frustrated. His life teaches us that we cannot change what happens – it happens for various reasons – but we *can* change our reaction to it. The message of His life is "adapt and adjust." Move forward. We cannot stop the wind from blowing, but we can change the direction of our sails, so that instead of capsizing our boat, we use the wind to take us to our destination.

Departure Alone in the Jungle, Even for the King

Even at the time of Lord Krishna's *Lila Sanvarana* (departure from the Earthly realm), shot by an arrow from a hunter's bow, deep in the secluded forest, He was full of divine light and compassion, forgiving the guilt-ridden hunter. Never did He bemoan the ending of His life on Earth, nor did He cry out for help from His thousands of subjects and devotees. Instead, He consoled the guilt-ridden hunter and quietly left the Earth, alone in the jungle, miles and miles from the glorious kingdom of Dwarka.

We may be "kings" in this lifetime, living in palaces of gold, but at the end we are always alone. We must cross the threshold from this life to the next alone. Therefore, it matters not what riches we acquire, nor what status we hold. None of it can save us from the hunter's arrow. None of it can come to our rescue at the time of death. All that matters is how we have lived our lives, whom we have helped, whom we have healed, and to whom we have brought peace and comfort.

Although Lord Krishna departed from the Earth on that day in the jungle, He is always with us, living on and on in our hearts, minds and souls. He is ever-present, all-knowing and all-powerful.

Seeing Bhagwan Krishna Everywhere

A very important message from Bhagwan Krishna's life is to see Him everywhere, in everyone, all the time. He is embodied in every form and in all forms. In Lord Krishna's childhood, he gave Mother Yasoda the *darshan* of the entire world in His mouth. Everything was shown to her in Lord Krishna's mouth. When we sit in our *puja*, in our worship/meditation we look at God's divine image and we see everything in Him. However, we must go further than just seeing everything in God. We must also see God in everything! When we look at a poor child, or when we look at an old widow, or when we look in the face of our enemy, we must see God. Then we will truly have learned the message of Bhagwan Krishna's teachings.

The Ultimate Divine Message

As we celebrate the divine occasion of Lord Krishna's appearance day, let us remember to take to heart the message of His life: *never lose yourself due to external circumstances, never lose your smile, never lose your song…*

Let us offer to Him, on this sacred day, not only our prayers and our *aarti*, but let us offer our lives at His holy feet, so that we, too, may become divine, pure and ever blissful.

Raksha Badhan:
A Festival of Love, Affection,
& Protection

The holiday of Raksha Bandhan, or Rakhi, is a celebration of the bond of love and the bond of family. It is celebrated on the full moon day of the month of Shravana (August - September). On this day, sisters tie sacred threads around their brothers' wrists, symbolizing their love and affection. In return, the brother promises to protect his sister and to always be there for her. *Raksha* means protection or security and *bandhan* means a bond or relation. Thus, Raksha Bandhan symbolizes the bond of security and protection between brothers and sisters.

As the *rakhi* is tied, a sacred mantra is chanted which says:

Yena baddho bali raajaa daanavendro mahaabalah
Tena twaam anubadhnaami rakshey maa chala maa chala.

This is a sacred protection mantra and it grants security and protection to the wearer.

In the South, Raksha Bandhan is celebrated by the Brahmins who put on a new sacred thread on this day.

Indian Culture – The World is One Family

On Rakhi, the brothers and sisters do not have to be blood relatives. That is the beauty of Indian culture. Our tradition tells us that everyone in the world is our brother and sister. On this day of Raksha Bandhan, a girl can tie a *rakhi* on the wrist of any boy or man to whom she feels a close bond. Then, from that day forth, they will call each other "sister" and "brother." In this way, relationships are strengthened, solidified and purified. The tradition of Raksha Bandhan symbolizes and underscores the way Indians live together as brother and sister – relationships filled with love, devotion and affection, but free from lust, attraction or violence.

The Bond of Rakhi

Additionally, the tradition of Rakhi has created a beautiful, sacred way for women and girls to be protected during times of political and social turmoil. Even as men injure and dishonor women, no one would injure his own sister. The bond of Rakhi is held so sacred that no man would dare leave his rakhi sister unprotected, let alone actually injure her himself. For example, the ancient Muslim ruler of India, Humayun, was obligated to protect the Hindu princess Karmavati, even in spite of all political and social sanctions against Karmavati and her family. Why? Because the princess had sent Humayun a *rakhi*.

Sacred Beginning

The holiday, like all Indian festivals, has a divine, sacred beginning. During the time of the *Mahabharata*, Lord Krishna threw a celestial weapon at Shishupala in order to punish him for his numerous sins. However, as Lord Krishna hurled the weapon at Shishupala, the Lord cut his own finger. Draupadi immediately tore off a piece from her sari and wrapped it around Lord Krishna's finger, stopping the bleeding. Lord Krishna asked her what she wanted in return for this favor. "Nothing, Oh Lord," she replied. "Just your holy presence in my life, at all times." So, from that moment forth, Lord Krishna promised Draupadi that He would always be with her and that she needed only to call upon Him. Later, as the Kauravas tried to dishonor Draupadi by removing her *sari* in a public hall, she called to Lord Krishna who immediately came to her rescue.

Bond With God

The story above about Bhagwan Krishna and Draupadi shows us more than simply the bond between a brother and sister or the promise of security. This teaches us a valuable lesson about our own relationship with God. Draupadi gave to Lord Krishna one small strand from her *sari*. In return, Lord Krishna gave Draupadi an endless, infinite *sari*, one which could never be removed. When we come forward toward the Lord, even one small step, He comes toward us by miles. When we offer one small strand of our lives at His holy feet, the rewards are infinite.

New Millennium, New Tradition

On this holy day of Raksha Bandhan there is so much to learn, so many vows to make. First, there are the ancient, traditional meanings, whereby girls and women remember their brothers – far and near – with love and affection. In exchange, all men and boys promise to protect their sisters – both against physical harm, and also against dishonor to their name or to their family. These are as crucial today as they were in the past.

However, perhaps even more importantly, we must realize that the only way the current world will survive is united as one family. Thus, now, we must also take the deeper, underlying meaning of Rakhi. We must vow to make the world our brothers and sisters – not only in theory, but also in practice. Let us use *rakhi* as a symbol of our universal brotherhood. May our girls and women lead the way toward this universal family as they tie *rakhi* bracelets on the wrists of not only their closest male friends, but also on the wrists of enemies. Let us use this holiday to reach out to those around us, embracing them as brother and sister.

Additionally, in this world in which relations between boys and girls are becoming more and more promiscuous, let us use *rakhi* to re-purify our relations. As girls and women tie *rakhi* bracelets on the wrists of boys and men who are their friends, may all of their minds become purified of any lustful feelings by this new, sanctified relationship of "sister" and "brother."

The True Raksha Bandhan

Last and most importantly, may we all exchange vows of love, affection and protection not only with our human brothers and sisters. Let us also offer at least a small thread to the Lord, for He is our true Brother, our true Sister, our true Protector. It is to Him that we want to be eternally tied. The divine *rakhi* that you offer to the Lord will never become untied, never become faded and will never break.

Navaratri

The festival of Navaratri is a glorious time of the year, filled with joy, celebration, and great lessons for our lives. *Navaratri* means "nine nights." This festival occurs twice a year, at the change from winter to summer in the Spring, and again at the change from summer to winter in the Autumn. The Autumn festival is celebrated from the first day to the ninth day of the bright half of Ashvina (September-October), while the Spring Festival is celebrated in Chaitra (April - May). The two Navaratri celebrations are known as Rama-Navaratri in Chaitra and Durga Navaratri in Ashvina. The celebration of Navaratri is in honor of the great Mother Goddess. The festival lasts for nine days, signifying the nine glorious aspects of the Divine Mother.

Additionally, during the time of Navratri and Dusshera, particularly in the state of Gujarat, there is a special tradition of Garba dancing. This is a special type of group dance which is typically performed in a circle, along with clapping of the hands or of sticks. Garba dancing is typically performed at night, in an open space, and it is believed that not only is the dance *to* the Mother Goddess, but also that the Mother Goddess is *part* of the dance itself, and that the dancers are dancing with Her.

There are different *pujas* and ceremonies performed on each of the nine days, most notably fasting on the eighth day and then immersion of Goddess Durga's image in holy rivers on Dusshera, which falls on the day right after Navratri ends (the 10th day).

Indian tradition is one of the few traditions in which the Feminine aspect of the divine is worshipped with as much reverence as the Masculine aspect. Throughout India you will see thousands of temples dedicated to various manifestations of the Divine Mother. You will find hundreds of thousands of people who are "*Shakti* worshippers."

Shakti is the energy of the Lord. Without the divine *Shakti*, even God is powerless. The creative aspect (Lord Brahma), the sustaining aspect (Lord Vishnu) and the destructive aspect (Lord Shiva) all have their respective *Shaktis* who provide the cosmic energy and omnipotent power needed for these great feats.

Additionally, everything for which we pray – knowledge, prosperity, love – are manifest in the Divine Feminine. Goddess Saraswati is the Goddess of knowledge. Maha Laxmi is the Goddess of prosperity. This shows that without the Divine Mother, our prayers would be in vain, and our wishes would go unanswered.

So, Navaratri is the time of worship of the Divine Mother. Beautiful *pujas, havans* and *aartis* are performed for Her. Through singing Her glories we pray that She will purify our lives and bring us health, happiness, peace and prosperity.

Navratri is celebrated as the time that Goddess Durga (Shakti) conquered the evil demon, Mahishasura, thereby saving the world from his vicious tyranny. It is said that Mahishasura was reigning terror over the world and none of the gods was able to destroy him. Thus, they all approached Goddess Durga – also known as Shakti – together and gave Her their weapons. Thus armed with Divine Shakti and the most powerful weapons, She conquered the demon and ended his tyranny after fighting for nine straight nights. On the tenth day, Vijaya Dasami, the demon was slaughtered.

This victory, and other beautiful stories associated with Goddess Durga, are celebrated with great fervor throughout different parts of India. *Shakti puja* is performed in elaborate and lavish ways.

The nine days of the festival also represent the three stages through which one passes on the spiritual path. During the first three days, the Mother is worshipped in her powerful, destructive, terrifying aspect. Many people, when beginning the spiritual path, have an inherent fear of God; therefore this first phase of Navaratri represents the first stage of a spiritual path. During these three days, the devotee prays to the Mother to use Her destructive power to destroy their imperfections and their faults. He prays for Her to make him pure enough to receive the divine energy. Additionally, this terrifying aspect of the Divine is the one who protects the new spiritual seeker on his path. Thus, the first three days of Navratri are devoted to annihilating the negative tendencies of our minds and hearts.

The second three days of Navaratri are days in which the Mother is worshipped in Her prosperity-bestowing form. Once the negative tendencies have been annihilated, one is ready to begin developing a positive, spiritual personality. These are the days that positive attributes replace the negative attributes which were removed. These days are the worship of Maha Lakshmi, the bestower of prosperity. On the spiritual path, after people overcome the fear of God, they frequently pray for material wealth or external prosperity. They pray for success in their ventures and for the removal of obstructions in their path. The prosperity Maha Laxmi bestows is not merely material prosperity, but it is also all of the qualities which a sincere spiritual seeker craves – calmness, peace, equanimity, compassion, and love.

During the last three days, Goddess Saraswati is worshipped as the bestower of true wisdom and understanding. Once the devotee has been purified by Goddess Durga and has had his vices annihilated, and once he has had the spiritual wealth of inner peace, calmness, compassion and love bestowed upon him by Maha Laxmi, then he is ready to receive the true light of understanding. This wisdom can not come unless the devotee has passed through the first two stages. Just as one would not pour divine nectar into an unclean, broken and impure cup, one can similarly not expect to have divine wisdom granted unless the vessel has been purified and made divine.

Frequently on the spiritual path, seekers wish to attain divine knowledge without first purifying themselves and attaining positive qualities. This is impossible, however.

The true light of Divine Wisdom can only be bestowed once the seeker has annihilated his negative tendencies and begun to develop a positive, spiritual attitude.

Therefore, Navarati should be a time of not only celebrating Goddess Durga's triumph over the evil demon, but rather it should also be a time of praying to Goddess Durga to remove the evil from within us. We must pray to her to annihilate our inner enemies – our ego, our greed, our anger – just as she vanquished the evil demon. These traits inside us are just as powerful, just as insidious, and just as deadly as any of the *asuras* or *rakshasas*.

Let us note also that Goddess Durga wears red, which symbolizes divine action. The Goddess is never idle. She is always busy in the destruction of evil in the world. As we vow to remove the evil from our own hearts and our own lives, we must be just as vigilant, just as active and just as conscientious. We must never become complacent; for anger, greed, ego, and lust are always present, always lurking, always ready to make home in welcoming hearts.

Dussehra

The day after Navratri (frequently referred to as the tenth day of Navratri) is Dusshera, which commemorates the day on which the ten-headed demon, Ravana, was killed. On this day, Bhagwan Rama defeated the ten-headed Ravana, thereby rescuing His wife Sitaji who had been kidnapped by this evil ruler of Lanka. The story of the war and Lord Rama's victory is re-enacted with great fervor on this holiday.

There is a beautiful tradition of *Rama-Lila*, which is the story of Bhagwan Rama being acted out, along with song and dance. People love to watch the victory of Bhagwan Rama over Ravana and to celebrate the safe return of Sitaji.

However, embedded within this scriptural epic are vital messages for our lives today. We must not let the deeper lessons and meaning get overshadowed by the joyous festivities of the day.

The word *"Dusshera"* means cutting off the ten heads of Ravana, or symbolically of our ego. The ten heads represent passion, pride, anger, greed, infatuation, lust, hatred, jealousy, selfishness and crookedness.

As we celebrate this holiday, as we revel in Lord Rama's victory, let us ask ourselves, "Has the Rama in us been victorious over our own Ravana? Is the good in our hearts conquering the evil? Have we decapitated the ten-headed demon within us?" Have we annihilated passion, pride, anger, greed, infatuation, lust, hatred, jealousy, selfishness and crookedness from our own lives?

Dussehra is not only a *holiday* about Lord Rama and the demon Ravana. It is a *holy day* about examining ourselves. When faced with a choice of how to act, do we act like Rama or like Ravana?

After the battle in Lanka, when Lord Rama was showing Sitaji the battlefield, He did not say, "This is where I slaughtered the evil Ravana." Rather, He said, "This is where Ravana died." Even after achieving the momentous task of killing the demon, Lord Rama was still humble. On the other hand, in our own lives we usually crave the attention, the praise and the respect of others. We are so quick to point out our own achievements. We are so quick to put ourselves in the center. Let us take this beautiful lesson of how to remain humble, pious and selfless. "This is where Ravana died," not, "This is where I bravely conquered Ravana."

Also, while Ravana lay dying, Bhagwan Rama did not revel in the victory. Rather, He sent His brother Lakshman to learn from the dying demon. For, Ravana was a great, peerless scholar of the Vedas who through his own ego, pride, vanity and insatiable desires became a demon. So, Bhagwan Rama sent Lakshman to go and listen to words of wisdom from Ravana as the latter lay on his death bed. Bhagwan

---

Rama knew that, although Ravana's vices had brought about his downfall, he still was a venerable scholar and one from whom great wisdom could be attained.

Further, remember that the war was won because Rama had built a bridge to Lanka, a bridge to the enemy. This is also an important lesson. In our lives we should learn to build bridges between ourselves and others, even with those whom we may consider enemies. Rather than isolating ourselves from others, let us learn to build bridges.

So, on this day in which we celebrate the demise of Ravana, let us ask ourselves if our inner Ravana is dead as well. Let us pledge to remove the evil ten-headed demon from our own lives. Let us pray to God for the strength to be selfless, pure, humble, loving and honest every day of our lives. Let us take steps *each day* (not only on Dussehra) to become more and more like Lord Rama. Let us build bridges between ourselves and others.

At the end of every day, when we introspect and examine our actions, our thoughts and our words, let us open our balance sheets and see whether we are acting more like Rama or more like Ravana. Let us vow that we will strive to bring forth the inner Rama and to vanquish the inner Ravana.

Diwali

The time of Diwali is one of the most festive and beautiful times of the year. *"Diwali"* literally means "A Row of Lights." It is a time filled with light and love; a time when Indians all over the world rejoice. Diwali is celebrated on the thirteenth/fourteenth day in the dark half of Kartik (October - November). It is also known as Krishna Chaturdashi. It is the darkest night of the darkest period, yet it is a celebration of light! Diwali is heralded as the triumph of good over evil.

The meanings of Diwali, its symbols and rituals, and the reasons for celebration are innumerable. Diwali celebrates Lord Rama's glorious and long-awaited return to his Kingdom of Ayodhya after his fourteen long years of exile in the forests. It commemorates Lord Krishna's victory over the demon Narakaasura who had kidnapped and terrorized the *gopis* of Vrindavan. When the evil Naraka was finally killed by Bhagwan Krishna and Satyabhaama, he begged pitifully for mercy; thus, upon his entreaties, it was declared that this day of his death would be celebrated with great joy and festivity. It is also celebrated as the day Bhagwan Vishnu married Maha Lakshmi.

Diwali is also associated with the story of the fall of Bali – a demon king who was conquered by Lord Vishnu. Lord

Vishnu appeared to the demon king Bali in the form of a dwarf and requested only three steps of land. The evil and egotistic Bali granted the drawf's meager request of only three feet. Suddenly, Lord Vishnu took on His grand size and placed one foot on the Earth, another on the Heavens and His third on the head of the evil Bali.

In general, Diwali signifies the triumph of good over evil, of righteousness over treachery, of truth over falsehood, and of light over darkness.

Additionally, Diwali is the holy time in which we offer our prayers to Maha Lakshmi and we worship Her with piety and devotion. Maha Lakshmi is the goddess of wealth and prosperity, bestowing these abundantly upon her devotees.

Diwali is a holiday of joy; it is the time when we gather with loved ones, celebrating our family, our friends and the prosperity God has bestowed upon us.

However, it is also a holiday that is widely misunderstood and misrepresented, especially in the West. I have heard that in the West Diwali is referred to as "The Indians' Christmas" and that it is celebrated with frivolity and decadence. Let us talk about what Diwali really means, about why we celebrate it and about why we worship Goddess Lakshmi on this day.

Celebration of Light

There are three main aspects of this holiday called Diwali.

The first is the celebration of light. We line our homes and streets with lanterns; we explode fireworks; children play with sparklers.

However, Diwali is not a festival of light in order that we may burn candles, fireworks and sparklers. Sure, these are wonderful ways of expressing our gaiety. But, they are not the only or true meaning of "light." Diwali is a festival of the light which dispels the darkness of our ignorance; it is a festival of the light which shows us the way on our journey through life. The purpose is not to glorify the light of the candle, or the light of the firecracker. The purpose is to glorify the light of God. It is He who bestows the real light, the everlasting light upon the darkness of this mundane world. A candle burns out. A firework is a momentary visual experience. But, the candle of a still mind and the fireworks of a heart filled with *bhakti* are divine and eternal; these are what we should be celebrating.

We decorate our homes with lanterns, but why? What is the symbolism behind that? Those lanterns signify God's light, penetrating through the ignorance and sin of our daily lives. Those lanterns signify the divine light, shining its way through this mundane world. A home bathed in light is a home in which anger, pain, and ignorance are being dispelled; it is a home that is calling to God. However, too many people turn this into a domestic beauty contest, spending days and a great deal of money to purchase the newest *dias*, the most beautiful candles. "We had seventy-five candles burning last night," we gloat. This is only the light of glamour. It is not the light of God, and thus the true meaning of the holiday is lost.

The light of Diwali should be within us. It should symbolize the personal relationship between God and our families. It should not be so we attract attention from passing cars, or so we are the envy of the neighborhood. Let the light penetrate inward, for only there will it have lasting benefit. One piece of cotton soaked in ghee, lit with a pure heart, a conscious mind and an earnest desire to be free from ignorance is far "brighter" than one hundred fashion *deepaks*, lit in simple unconscious revelry.

A Fresh Start

Diwali also marks the new year. For some, the day of Diwali itself is the first day of the new year, and for others the new year's day is the day following Diwali. But, for all this season is one of heralding in the New Year.

In the joyous mood of this season, we clean our homes, our offices, our rooms, letting the light of Diwali enter all the corners of our lives. We begin new checkbooks, diaries and calendars. It is a day of "starting fresh."

On this day we clean every room of the house, we dust every corner of the garage, we sweep behind bookshelves, vacuum under beds and empty out cabinets. But, what about our hearts? When was the last time we swept out our hearts? When did we last empty them of all the dirt and garbage that has accumulated throughout our lives?

That is the real cleaning we must do. That is the real

meaning of "starting fresh." We must clean out our hearts, ridding them of darkness and bitterness; we must make them clean and sparkling places for God to live. We must be as thorough with ourselves as we are with our homes. Are there any dark corners in our hearts we have avoided for so long? Are we simply "sweeping all the dirt under the rug"? God sees all and knows all. He knows what is behind every wall of our hearts, what is swept into every corner, and what is hidden under every rug. Let us truly clean out our hearts; let us rid ourselves of the grudges, pain, and anger that clutter our ability to love freely. Let us empty out every nook and cranny, so that His divine light can shine throughout.

Additionally, on Diwali, we begin a new checkbook; we put last year's accounts to rest. But, what about our own balance sheets? When was the last time we assessed our minuses and plusses, our strengths and our weaknesses, our good deeds and selfish deeds? How many years' worth of grudges and bitterness and pain have we left unchecked?

A good businessman always checks his balance sheet: how much he spent, how much he earned. A good teacher always checks the progress of her students: how many are passing, how many are failing? Then they assess themselves accordingly: "Am I a good businessman?" "Am I a good teacher?" In the same way we must assess the balance sheets of our lives. Look at the last year. Where do we stand? How many people did we hurt? How many did we heal? How many times did we lose our temper? How many times did we give more than we received? Then, just as we give our past checkbooks and the first check of our new one to God, let us give all our minus and plus points to Him. He is the one responsible for all our good deeds. Our bad ones are due only to ignorance. So, let us turn everything over to Him, putting our strengths, our weaknesses, our wins and our losses at His holy feet. And then, let us start afresh, with a new book, unadulterated by old grudges and bitterness.

Maha Lakshmi

The third, and perhaps most important, aspect of Diwali is the worship of Maha Lakshmi. Maha Lakshmi is the goddess of wealth and prosperity, bestowing these abundantly upon her devotees. On Diwali we pray to her for prosperity; we ask her to lavish us with her blessings. However, what sort of prosperity are we praying for? All too often, we infer wealth to mean money, possessions, and material pleasures. This is *not* the true wealth in life; this is not what makes us prosperous. There is almost no correlation between the amount of money we earn, the number of possessions we buy, and our sense of inner bliss and prosperity.

It is only God's presence in our lives which makes us rich. Look at India. People in small villages, in holy towns, in ancient cities have very little in terms of material possessions. Most of them live below the Western standards of poverty. Yet, if you tell them they are poor, they won't believe you, for in their opinion they are not. This is because they have God at the center of their lives. Their homes may not have TV sets, but they all have small *mandirs*; the children may not know the words to the latest rock-and-roll song, but they know the words to *Aarti*; they may not have computers or fancy history text books, but they know the stories of the *Ramayana*, the *Mahabharata* and other holy scriptures; they may not begin their days with newspapers, but they begin with prayer.

If you go to these villages, you may see what looks like poverty to you. But, if you look a little closer, you will see that these people have a light shining in their eyes, a glow on their faces and a song in their hearts that money cannot buy.

On Diwali, we must pray to Maha Lakshmi to bestow real prosperity upon us, the prosperity that brings light to our lives and sparkle to our eyes. We must pray for an abundance of faith, not money; we must pray for success in our spiritual lives, not a promotion at work; we must pray for the love of God, not the love of the beautiful girl (or boy) in our class.

There is another point about Maha Lakshmi that is important. We tend to worship only her most prominent of aspects – that of bestowing prosperity upon her devotees. However, she is a multi-faceted goddess, filled with symbols of great importance. As we worship her, let us look more deeply at her divine aspects. First, according to our scriptures, she is the divine partner of Lord Vishnu. In Hindu tradition, there is almost always a pair – a male and a female manifestation of the Divine –who play inter-dependent roles. It is said that Maha Lakshmi provides

Lord Vishnu with the wealth necessary in order to sustain life. He sustains, but through the wealth she provides.

Therefore, in its highest meaning, Maha Lakshmi provides wealth for sustenance, not for indulgence. Our material wealth and prosperity should only sustain us, giving us that which is necessary to preserve our lives. All surplus should be used for humanitarian causes. She does not give wealth so that we may become fat and lazy; yet, that is what we tend to do with the wealth we receive. Let us remember that Maha Lakshmi's material wealth is meant for sustenance and preservation, not for luxury and decadence.

Additionally, we worship Maha Lakshmi who is the divine symbol of purity and chastity. Yet, in our celebration of her, we frequently indulge in frivolity and hedonism. How can we worship her while engaging in the opposite of what she represents? We must re-assess how we pay tribute to this holy Goddess.

The last point I want to mention is that she is typically portrayed wearing red. What does this mean? Red is the color of action, and she is the goddess of prosperity. This means that in order to obtain the true prosperity in life, we must engage in action. Most people think that in order to be spiritual, or to obtain "spiritual prosperity," one must be sitting in lotus posture in the Himalayas. This is not the only way. In the *Bhagavad Gita*, Lord Krishna teaches about *Karma Yoga*, about serving God by doing your duty. We must engage ourselves in active, good service; that is truly the way to be with Him.

Let our inner world be filled with devotion to Him, and let our outer performance be filled with perfect work, perfect action. I once heard a story about a man who spent forty years meditating so he could walk on water. He thought that if he could walk on water, then he had truly attained spiritual perfection. When I heard this story, I thought, "Why not spend forty cents instead for a ride in the motorboat across the river, and spend the forty years giving something to the world?" That is the real purpose of life.

So, on this holy day, let us fill our entire beings with the light of God. Let us clean out our minds and hearts, making a true "fresh start." Let us pray to Maha Lakshmi to bestow the divine gifts of faith, purity and devotion upon us. With those, we will always be always rich, always prosperous, and always fulfilled. Let us celebrate Diwali this year as a true "holy day," not only as another frivolous "holiday."

Thanksgiving

By Sadhvi Bhagwati

In America, one of the biggest holidays of the year is Thanksgiving. The feast is in honor of the first good harvest after the pilgrims came to the new land.

In theory, this holiday is a beautiful one. The idea of gathering to give thanks, gathering on behalf of the bountiful harvest God has provided, gathering with family, is wonderful. It is one of the few times a year that Americans tend to ensure that the entire family is together. Thus, in this regard Thanksgiving is a great, wonderful tradition.

However, unfortunately, the hallmark of this holiday is a large, roasted turkey sitting as the centerpiece on a beautifully decorated table, just waiting to be carved by the family members and relished with a side of potatoes and cranberries!

When I was a child, my family would always fly from Los Angeles to New York for Thanksgiving. We would gather with my grandparents, aunts, uncles, cousins and friends. Before we began eating the many-course feast that sat, steaming, on the table in front of us, we would go around, each of us saying one thing we were thankful for. "I'm thankful I'm not a turkey," I used to say. Year after year my grandfather would admonish me as soon as we entered the New England home. He'd stare down at me and demand to know, "You're not going to say it again this year are you? You've outgrown that stupid little trick, haven't you?" And each year I would lovingly reassure him that, no, I would not say it again. I would soothe his concern and tell him that I would say something "appropriate" this year.

Yet, as we sat – a family for whom expense was not an issue, a family who were not hunter/gatherers having to live only on that which they could pick or kill – around a huge, oval table, in a posh country home on the shore of the Atlantic ocean, I could think of nothing but the life lost by the large animal on the table in front of me.

We gather each November in the name of thanks. We gather to appreciate the bountiful harvest, to savor the wealth of the land called America. Yet, how can we simultaneously sit – with bowed heads – thanking a land whose creatures we slaughter? How can we give thanks for life, while consuming the life of another? How can we thank God for freedom when the food on our plates has spent its entire life in captivity, waiting to become a "roast"?

I realize these are harsh questions. I pray to God for the ability to ask them gently. Yet, it seems to me that the situation is severe enough, the suffering great enough, and our blindness complete enough that these questions must be asked. I feel that the meat industry in the West has all the propaganda weapons at its disposal: all the publicity, all the man-power, all the lobbyists. But, on the other side lies the truth; so, if it is all we have, we must not be afraid to face this truth.

From the time I was a child – long before I became a vegetarian – eating meat never felt quite right to me. I would only eat boneless meat, hidden in sauce, or already cut up meat, put into sandwiches. I could never bear to cut my food from its bone. But, I lived in a society where to refuse meat (especially as a child) incurred such a barrage of questions and criticisms that I was reluctant to do so.

When I was fifteen however, something happened that changed not only my eating habits but my entire vision of the American diet. I read a book called *Diet for a New America*, written by a man named John Robbins. Robbins was the eldest son of Mr. Robbins, from the Baskin-Robbins ice cream fortune, and had been slated to inherit this multi-million dollar corporation. But, he was a man of truth, and he decided that he could not in good conscience condone the way these dairy cows were treated. Ten years of seclusion and meditation later, he returned to America to make a thorough investigation of the meat and dairy industries and to unveil the travesties buried within. The book makes the most compelling case I have ever seen for vegetarianism. It is so filled with truth, love and wisdom that it gave me the courage to live by what my heart felt was right. The day I read the book was the last day I ate any form of meat or meat products. I became a young, stubborn vegetarian in a society that adamantly tried to convince me I was depriving myself of both nutrients and enjoyment. However, knowing that I was acting from my heart gave me a window of truth through which to look at the world.

It feels to me that the way in which we Westerners celebrate, the way in which we give thanks does not have a lot of integrity. Perhaps we really are thankful; perhaps our hearts are honestly filled with joyous celebration. Nonetheless our actions – having a roast turkey as the star of this holiday – do not seem to me to be in concert with feelings of deep gratitude.

I look at the way Indians give thanks, at what symbols and rituals pervade their *puja*. I look at a *yagna*. The spirit of *yagna* is sacrifice. These celebrations are not filled with sensual gratification at the expense of others. Rather, they are filled with a true spirit of thanks: God has given to us, so our heart says we should sacrifice for Him, give back to Him. The symbols of a *yagna* – the burning of our sins and desires, the offering of everything at the holy feet of the Lord – this is what feels to me like true thanks. Those who are full of blessings, and gratitude for those blessings, have a natural instinct to share with others. It seems, in contrast, that there is something reprehensible about the idea of sitting down to thank God through the consumption of His child smothered in gravy!

Let us, instead, pause and give thanks for something far more valuable than a bountiful harvest. Let us give thanks for our human ability to have compassion, to have empathy for the plight of another, to make choices that not only satisfy our bodies in the moment, but that satisfy our hearts and souls. Let us, rather than destroy our precious environment and the creatures who live within it, let us give thanks for the land that can feed us, feed our fellow creatures, convert carbon dioxide into oxygen, give us medicine to heal our sickness and provide shelter for all God's creatures.

Let us give thanks for our ability to think clearly, to discriminate between right and wrong, and to sacrifice a temporary pleasure for the benefit of another. Let us give thanks for our ability to choose right from wrong and our freedom to act accordingly.

Gita Jayanti

Gita Jayanti is celebrated on the 11th day (*Ekadashi*) of the bright fortnight of the month of Margaseersha (December – January). Sometimes people refer to it as the "Birthday of the *Bhagavad Gita*"; however, divine wisdom cannot be said to take birth! One cannot really say that the *Divine Song* has a birthday. Gita Jayanti is the anniversary of the day, nearly 6000 years ago, when Sanjaya recited the words which Bhagwan Shri Krishna spoke to Arjuna on the battlefield of Kurukshetra for the blind King Dhritarashtra. Along with the epic of the *Mahabharata*, this *Divine Song* was transcribed into words by Veda Vyasji for the benefit of humanity.

Paramhansa Yogananda (one of the great spiritual leaders of India who spread the message of the *Gita* to the West) said, "The *Bhagavad Gita* is the most beloved scripture of India, a scripture of scriptures. It is the Hindu's *Holy Testament*, the one book that all masters depend upon as a supreme source of scriptural authority." The *Gita* provides wisdom and upliftment, comfort and solace to people of all ages, from all walks of life and from all corners of the Earth.

"*Bhagavad Gita*" literally means "Song of God, Song of the Soul, Song of the Spirit." Like any truly divine song, the language of the original lyrics and the religion of the original singer are irrelevant. For once it has been written and sung, the song itself becomes alive, bursting forth across oceans and mountain ranges, breaking all barriers of caste, creed, and nationality. Such is the power of a divine song. However, since the original "singer" of the *Gita* is Bhagwan Shri Krishna Himself, this is one of the holiest and most sacred songs of God. Its power to transform, to heal, and to uplift is as limitless as the Singer.

Mahatma Gandhiji said, "When disappointment stares me in the face and all alone I see not one ray of light, I go back to the *Bhagavad Gita*...I immediately begin to smile in the midst of overwhelming tragedies, and my life has been full of external tragedies. If they have left no visible, no indelible scar on me, I owe it all to the teachings of *Bhagavad Gita*."

The *Gita* consists of 700 shlokas divided into eighteen chapters. It has been said that the *Upanishads* are the cows, Krishna is the cowherd, Arjuna is the calf, and the *Gita* is the milk. But, it is not just any milk. This milk is nectar that flowed from God with the power to heal the sick, comfort the lonely, guide the lost, uplift the fallen and bring peace to the troubled. The milk is gentle and pure enough for a baby, but strong enough for a warrior.

The *Gita* was spoken as Arjuna surveyed the battlefield of Kurukshetra. Upon seeing the opposing army, the great warrior suddenly became dismayed and despondent, laying down his arms. He told Krishna that he could not fight. "I see in the opposing army my cousins, my uncles, my revered teachers. It would be better to renounce the kingdom than to fight with those who are so close to me," he bemoaned. Thus began the *Bhagavad Gita*.

Lord Krishna took Arjuna on the journey from despondency to devotion – devotion to God and devotion to his own *dharma*. That is the divine gift of the *Gita*: to carry us from a state of despair to a state of joy.

The teachings of the *Gita* however are not applicable merely to life on a battlefield, when war with our relatives is imminent. Rather the true battlefield is within us. Through the story of Arjuna and the battle, Bhagwan Shri Krishna gives us lessons for our lives. The real Kurukshetra is within us. Each of us is Arjuna, struggling with right and wrong, temptation, fear and frustration. Our bodies are our chariots, being driven all too frequently by our senses as the horses. The mind, ego, desires, lust and greed are the evil Kauravas with whom we must do righteous battle, from whom we must not shy away in fear. If we give the reins of our lives to God (as Arjuna made Krishna his divine charioteer), we will surely be victorious.

If we, too want to transform our lives from despair and depression to devotion and delight we merely have to allow ourselves to be bathed in the *Bhagavad Gita*'s divine and healing powers.

The *Gita* is a "Map of Life," for it clearly shows us not

only the destination, but also the clearest and best path to reach there. Yet, like any good map, the *Gita* does not give us only one path. Rather, throughout the *Divine Song*, Bhagwan Krishna explains how – through devotion, through wisdom, and through action – one can reach the ultimate destination of union with God. For different temperaments He lays out different paths, all the while reminding us that true, earnest yearning and pure, sur-rendered love for God are the surest and simplest way to attain liberation.

The lessons of the *Gita* do not require one to be a great scholar or a great philosopher. Nor do they demand de-cades of exacting penance to earn God's favor. Rather, Bhagwan Krishna offers infinite and eternal comfort by His words, "Whoever comes to me with devotion will attain me."

A central message of the *Gita* is "Thou Art That;" we are all part and parcel of God. We are His divine children and He lives within us. To explicate this message, the *Gita* is divided into three sections, each of which goes into detail of one word of "Thou Art That."

The first section, made up of the first six chapters, details "Thou." This section is about who we are. It instructs us how to live, how to be, and the nature of our beings. This section is dedicated to *karma yoga*, the path of selfless service and action.

The second section details "That." This section talks about the nature of the Divine. It is dedicated to *bhakti yoga*, the path of devotion.

The third section explains "Art," the nature of being. It elucidates the connection between the individual soul and the Supreme Soul. It is the section dedicated to *jnana yoga*, the path of knowledge and wisdom.

The *Gita* explains that, although different people have different temperaments which are suited to different paths, ultimately the truth is one. The destination is one, although the paths may vary. So, the *Gita* does not espouse one path over another. Rather, it teaches us that each of the three paths leads to God, but that people should follow the path which is most suited to their own individual temperaments.

The Gita teaches us to be अस्त (*ast*), व्यस्त (*vyast*), मस्त (*mast*) and स्वस्थ (*swasth*). What do I mean? First, as we read the words, as the voice of Bhagwan Shri Krishna speaks to us, we become *ast*, emerged in God. The *Gita* becomes the blanket that wraps itself around us in the cold, dark of night. His words speak to us through the *Gita*, comforting us, teaching us and guiding us.

Then, as we study the message and the wisdom of the *Gita* more, we learn how to be *vyast*. *Vyast* — in essence —means "doing while being, and being while doing." This is Bhagwan Shri Krishna's message. So many people today assume that a spiritual path is one of idleness, one of silent contemplation high on a mountain top. But, Krishna teaches otherwise. We should be the hands that do God's work – this is *Karma Yoga*. We should not only be divine, but we should *do* divine. "Serve, serve, serve, do your duty on Earth." But, again, *vyast* is a different kind of "doing" than what most people do. It is "being" while "doing." What does this mean? It means having your work be prayer, having your work be meditation. The whole time your hands are doing, your mind should be being. Have His name be on your lips and in your heart, and have His work be on your hands.

From *ast* and *vyast*, we become *mast* – ever happy, ever joyful, ever blissful. When you are immersed in Him and His work is flowing through you, what else can you be? When you are *ast*, *vyast*, and *mast*, you automatically are *swasth* – completely healthy and in perfect balance. But *swasth* does not imply only perfect physical health; rather, it is a full health of body, mind, soul and spirit. Every pain, every ache, every discomfort becomes *prasad* as you lay it in His lap. His love and His presence dissolve all that hurts both within and without. Your body and your soul become in perfect harmony.

The central message of the *Gita* is to perform your duties diligently and piously, but without any expectation for what the result will be. You must till the soil, plant the seeds, water and tend the seedling, and take care of the tree without any thought of how much fruit this tree will bear. You must be God's gardener, carefully tending the garden but never becoming attached to what will blossom, what will flower, what will give fruit or what will wither and die. Expectation is the mother of frustration, but acceptance is the mother of peace and joy.

Bhagwan Shri Krishna says, "Stand up! Do divine! Be divine! Don't expect, but accept!" Life is about the journey, not about the destination. If the reins of your life-chariot are in His hands, you will be ever happy, ever peaceful. This is the lesson of ultimate surrender that we must take to heart. Put all your assets in the Divine Insurance Company, and you will always be taken care of.

The message of the *Gita* is as relevant for people living in India and also the West today as it was for the people of India more than 5000 years ago. It is as relevant for Hindus as for people of all other religions. It teaches Hindus how to be better Hindus, but it also teaches Muslims to be better Muslims, Christians to be better Christians, and Jews to be better Jews. For, if something is really "truth," it must be universal. Truth is not limited to a religious framework. If it is truth, it must pertain to all. Such is the profound truth of Bhagwan Shri Krishna's words.

Like Mother Ganga, like the rays of the sun, the *Bhagavad Gita* does not discriminate. Mother Ganga does not bring water to only Hindus' farms. The sun does not shine only on Hindus' flowers. Similarly, the *Gita* does not provide light and inspiration to only Hindus' minds and souls.

Aldous Huxley said, "The *Gita* is one of the clearest and most comprehensive summaries of the Perennial Philosophy ever to have been made. Hence its enduring value, not only for Indians, but for all mankind." Sometimes it seems that today people in the West actually need this wisdom even more than people in India. People in the West seem to hold even more tenaciously to their agendas, their expectations and their desires. The message in much of the West is, "If you work hard, you will succeed, you will become prosperous." So, people don't work for the sake of being God's hands. They work to reap the benefits, and when the benefits don't come or don't come quickly enough, they are frustrated.

The *Gita* provides the guiding principles for both peace in this life as well as for ultimate salvation. When I was in Japan, I saw a sign that said, "Follow the rules, and enjoy your stay." While it is simple and common, it is also profoundly true. The rules for our lives are laid out in the scriptures: do divine, be divine, serve without expectation, love all, hate none, heal all, hurt none, see the Divine in all, surrender to God, be honest, be humble, and remember that He is the real Do-er and we are only His tools.

When we follow these rules our lives overflow with joy, love, and peace. It is when we ignore these commandments or amend them to suit our own agendas that we bring pain and turmoil into our lives. The *Gita* is a complete yet concise listing of all the teachings ("rules") necessary to achieve Self-realization in this life as well as eternal salvation and liberation.

Additionally, because it was sung by Bhagwan Shri Krishna Himself, the *Gita* has the miraculous ability to give the reader exactly the answer and meaning he or she is searching for. So, if you open it today in the midst of a crisis at work you will come upon a passage that will speak something different to you than when you open it a year from now, looking for comfort after the death of a parent. Similarly, youth will find a different jewel in the treasure chest than adults will.

The *Bhagavad Gita* shows us the way to live with God, to live with each other and to live with Mother Earth in peace and harmony. This wisdom and insight is as changing as the River Ganga, able to address the concerns of each generation, yet as stable and everlasting as the Himalayas themselves.

It seems that people everywhere need both the message and the comfort of the *Gita* a great deal. The lives of people today seem colored by indelible scars. I hope they will all turn to the *Gita* as the remover of pain and the bestower of light.

Valentine's Day

In the Western world, February is the month of love, the month of Valentine's Day. Across the world, people spend billions of dollars on cards, chocolates, flowers, balloons and other external object to express their love. Although Valentine's Day is not a traditional Indian holiday, these days it has become almost universal.

On February 14th, we paint everything with pretty red hearts and say, "I love you. I love you. You are mine. I am yours. Be my Valentine." That is February 14th.

But, how are we on February 15th? Does that undying expression of love last even through the night? When our loved ones ask a favor on the 15th or the 16th of February, do we remember that we told them, "I am yours. You are mine," or do we revert back to our old patterns of selfishness and self-centeredness? We say these things with our tongues, but do we mean them with our hearts? It is our heart which must change, our heart which we must give to our beloved, not merely a box of chocolates. Valentine's Day is a holiday of the heart, but too frequently we make it only a holiday of the wallet.

The real way to celebrate Valentine's Day is to make every

day Valentine's Day. Make every day a day in which you give thanks for the loved ones in your life. Make every day a day in which you repeat, "I love you. I am yours. You are mine." Most importantly, make your heart and your actions match your words.

I have heard of a couple, married for fifty years who never had a fight, who never had a disagreement, and whose love at their 50th anniversary was as alive and magical as on the day they were married. To what did they attribute this success? Each morning before getting out of bed, they said to each other, "I love you and I am so lucky to begin this day by your side." Each night before sleeping they again said, "I love you and I am so lucky to end this day with you." Simple, easy, fast and free, yet how many of us could do this? Rather, we forget the simple, beautiful expressions of love and appreciation, and instead revert to material gifts and fancy dinners in the hope that this can make up for a dearth of true feeling. It cannot.

Further, we pour out our words of love to the people in our lives. We spend hours agonizing over what to buy them for this holiday, how best to express our feelings. But, who is our real Valentine? Who is the one who is always there for us, any time of any day, any day of the week? Who is the one who is always forgiving, always compassionate, and always willing to listen? Who is the one who never yells, never scolds, never calls us names? Who is the one whose arms are always open, who is always waiting for us? The answer is: our Divine Valentine, God. He is our real Valentine. Yet, how much time to we spend telling God, "I love you?" How much time do we spend with

Him? He is the only one who will never leave us, who will never betray us, who is always there for us.

I saw a sign once at a flower store in the USA on the day before Valentine's Day. It said, "Order Early. Buy one, get one free." God also tells us "Order Early." We must order Him as early as possible in our lives if we want to be filled with joy, peace and love. We must order Him early if we want our lives to be successful, meaningful and divine.

The flower shop says, "Buy one, get one free." God says, "Buy Me and be free!" If He is your Valentine, you will be free from pain, free from sorrow, and free from the chains that bind us to this mundane world.

Everyone else wants to know your history – where you come from, whom else you've loved, how much money you make, etc. But God says, "Just come to Me. I am yours." He doesn't care where you're from, whom else you've loved or how much you earn for salary. Once you make Him your valentine, He is yours completely. Then, you will never be lonely again.

I hear people who are unmarried, or who are widowed, or whose spouses are travelling say, "I don't have a Valentine." But, our true Valentine is always there. We came into the world in His arms, and it is to Him we will go when we die. So, let us open our arms and open our hearts to our true Valentine.

God doesn't care if we're wearing expensive perfume. He doesn't care if we have new shoes or a pretty haircut. He cares only about the purity of our hearts.

In the Ramayana (the story of Bhagwan Rama), the demon Ravana's sister (who was also evil) had a special boon of being remarkably, extraordinarily beautiful. Her name was Shurpanakha. She went to Bhagwan Rama and tried to seduce Him with her beauty. Her ultimate aim was to lure Him away through her seduction and guile.

However, Bhagwan Rama was not interested in superficial beauty. He could see straight through to her heart, and He knew that she was not pure on the inside. Thus, He firmly rebuked her advances.

On the other hand, there was Shabari. Shabari was a poor, illiterate, simple peasant woman, but her heart was divinely pure and devoted. She spent every day sweeping the entrance to her hut and the nearby streets of the villages in anticipation of the day that her God would come. She kept waiting, patiently, devotedly, purely, keeping her heart, her life and her hut clean and pure for God.

Whereas the beauty Shurpanakha had to travel to the abode of Bhagwan Rama in order to find Him and still she was rebuked, Shabari didn't even have to leave her hut. Bhagwan Rama came personally to her hut, knocked on her door, and asked for food.

When we become pure, devoted, holy, simple and pious, God comes to us, takes our hand and tells us, "You be my Valentine. I am here for you. I am your Valentine. I will always love you."

Shivratri

Shivaratri is one of the holiest nights of the year dedicated to the worship of Lord Shiva. Literally, *"Shivratri"* means "the great night of Shiva." It is celebrated on the 13th or 14th day of the dark half of the month of Phalguna (February - March).

In the trinity of gods – Brahma, Vishnu and Shiva – Lord Shiva is the one who destroys that which is old and impure in order to make room for a new creation that is pure and divine. Lord Shiva annihilates our egos, our attachments and our ignorance. Many fear Lord Shiva's destructive capacity, and yet it is destruction for the purpose of regeneration. Without death, life cannot begin anew. Without the annihilation of old habits, attachments and ego, we cannot progress toward the goal of God-realization. Unless our "vessel" has been emptied of all that is old, negative and impure, it cannot be filled with divine qualities.

The holiday of Shivratri is celebrated by performing special Shiva *puja* and *abhishek* as well as by remaining awake at night in meditation, *kirtan* and *japa*. During the course of the night, the *abhishek* can be performed every three hours with water, milk, yogurt, honey, and other such items. *Bel* (bilva) leaves are considered particularly auspicious to offer during Shiva *puja* and they are offered frequently, as it is believed that Maha Lakshmi resides within them. In fact, it is said that offering *bel* leaves on the occasion of Shivratri is so auspicious that even one who offers them unknowingly (as in the case of the hunter Suswara), one will attain liberation.

Bhagwan Shiva is portrayed with ash on his forehead, and devotees of Lord Shiva frequently apply sacred ash to various parts of their body. This symbolizes two things. Everything that today has a form on the Earth once was ash in the ground and again will be reduced to nothing but ash. Therefore, the ash serves to remind us that all that we are, all that we do, all that we earn and acquire will be reduced to ash one day, and therefore we should live our lives dedicated to God and dedicated to serving humanity, rather than to the accumulation of temporary possessions and comfort. When we apply the sacred ash or see it, we are reminded, "Ah yes, it is only by the grace of Lord Shiva that I am still here today, and that I have not yet been turned to ash. It is His grace that my home, my family and my possessions are still with me and that they have not become ash. Therefore, I should remember Him, pray to Him, and devote myself to Him."

The stories and the messages of Bhagwan Shiva are innumerable. One of the most important stories is of how He – for the sake of humanity – swallowed the poison which emerged from the ocean.

The story says that the devas and their brothers, the asuras or demons, were churning the ocean in search of the pot of the nectar of immortality. However, after a great deal of effort, what emerged was not nectar, but poison! This happens frequently in life as well. When we embark upon a divine plan or when we undertake a noble challenge, frequently before the success comes, before our effort bears fruit, we face failure or condemnation or seemingly insurmountable hurdles. Yet, we must never give up.

The devas and demons knew that in order to continue churning and ultimately unearth the Divine nectar, they could not simply toss the poison aside. Someone had to drink it. Naturally, no one was willing to drink the poison. Everyone had some excuse for why he or she was too valuable to be sacrificed. Finally, Bhagwan Shiva came forward, very calmly and with serene poise. He said, "I will drink the poison if it will preserve peace in the family and enable my brothers and sisters to attain the nectar of immortality."

After drinking the poison, and thereby enabling the churning to continue, Bhagwan Shiva held the poison in his throat – hence the name Neelkanth, or "Blue Throat" – and sat peacefully in meditation for eternity.

In our lives and in our families, so much poison emerges – between parents and children, between husband and wife, between in-laws. We wait and wait for the divine nectar to emerge, but it seems that only poison comes. So many times people come to me, complaining, "But why should I always be the one to compromise? Why should I always be the one to sacrifice? Why should I always say I'm sorry? It's not fair!"

On this night of Shivratri, as we worship Bhagwan Shiva, it is also the night that we must pray for the strength to take his message to heart! Let us not only worship him, but let us emulate him. He who is willing to peacefully swallow the poison, he who is willing to sacrifice for the family, for the community and for humanity, is the true Mahadeva.

Bhagwan Shiva went to the Himalayas, to the land now called Neelkanth to meditate after he drank the poison. The message is that when poison emerges in the home, when poison emerges anywhere in our lives, when we feel like if we swallow it we will die, but if we don't drink it then the fight will continue – the secret is to meditate! You don't have to go to the Himalayas. Just create your own Himalayas wherever you are. Be the one to accept the poison. Be the one to sacrifice, apologize and concede humbly. Then go sit and meditate peacefully. This is not weakness, but strength.

Poison always comes; obstacles always come. When we work for good causes, when we embark upon divine work, the poison always comes before the nectar. However, we must never get discouraged. We must never give up. If the devas and demons had forfeited the churning at the sign of poison, the nectar of immortality would never have emerged, and it would have been a tragedy for the world. Similarly, we must always have faith that the nectar *will* come. It is only a matter of time. We must be willing to churn and churn, no matter what comes – be it poison or nectar.

On the night of Shivratri as we remember the churning between the *devas* and demons for the nectar of immortality, we must take another lesson to heart. After the nectar emerged, the demons tried to run away with it so they would be even more powerful and able to destroy their brothers, the *devas*. However, through a series of divine interventions, the *devas* emerged the victors and the ones with the gift of immortality.

The night of Shivratri is especially auspicious for winning this same battle within ourselves – the battle between good and evil, between right and wrong, between poison and nectar, between death and immortality. Let us use our *puja*, our prayers, and our meditations on this night to pray for divine intervention so that within ourselves the good might vanquish the evil, the nectar within us might emerge rather than poison, and that we too may be carried from death to immortality.

Holi

Holi is one of the most festive, joyous holidays of the Hindu year. It is celebrated primarily in the North of India and falls on the full moon day of Phalguna (February - March). The festival is marked by great revelry during which everyone paints each other with brightly colored powders. Song, dance and bright red, green, yellow and pink powder are the hallmarks of the occasion.

The meanings of Holi are numerous. For some, it is the festival of Springtime, the heralding of warm weather and bidding farewell to the winter. It is also seen as a festival of love, the return of fertility and virility. However, side by side with the celebration of love and fertility is the messege to exercise control over the emerging passion. In some parts of India, the story is told on Holi of Kamadeva (God of Love; Cupid), whom Lord Shiva burned to ashes as he tried to seduce Him out of His meditation. The messege is: celebrate love, but don't get carried away. Thus, Holi is a celebration of divinity and discipline over passion.

The Puranas describe Holi as a celebration of virtue over vice. It is a time when we rejoice in the victory of pure, divine Prahlaad over his aunt Holika. The story says that Prahlaad was a young, beautiful, pure, divine devotee of God. However, Prah-laad's father was a powerful king who believed that everyone should worship him. At Prahlaad's refusal to do so due to his single-minded love of God, his father decided to have him killed. Prahlaad's aunt (his father's sister), Holika, had been given a special shawl as a boon from God for various austerities she had performed. When she wore this shawl, she could not be burned by fire. So, Prahlaad's father and his sister devised a plan in which she would wear her shawl and hold Prahlaad tightly in her arms as they sat in fire. In this way, Prahlaad would be killed, but she would emerge unscathed.

However, as the divine plan always works, a strong gust of wind came and blew the shawl off of her, as well as carried pure Prah-laad to safety. Holika was burned in the fire of her own evil.

One of the great obstacles in life to our spiritual progress is the difference between what we do or say on the outside and how we really are on the inside. Holika had performed certain austerities by which she was entitled to this boon from God. On the outside, she was "pious." But, on the inside, she was not pure. Prahlaad, on the other hand, was a simple, pure, loving devotee of God. This is what saved him. This inner purity and inner piety are what truly save us, what truly make our lives divine.

So many of us go to temple, do the rituals, offer money to the priests, and chant a certain number of rounds of our *malas*. Then, we go out and act in selfish, unpious, and dishonest ways. These may not necessarily take the form of malicious transgressions. It may simply be the way we speak to our children or to our loved ones. It may simply be the way we try to cheat those with whom we do business. It may be the way we sit and gossip about others.

All the rituals and *puja* in the world cannot make up for a lack of piety, honesty and compassion. The goal of going to temple is not just to perform rituals; the goal is to become spiritual. God is happier with pure, innocent, devoted Prahlaad than with all the austerities and rituals performed by his father and aunt.

Thus, on this divine occasion, we should pray to be filled with the purity and devotion of Prahlaad. We should commit ourselves to performing our *puja*, meditation and *japa* with focus, dedication and deep love for God.

One meaning of the word *"Holi"* is "sacrifice." On Holi we light many bonfires to revel in joy and to burn the effigies of Holika. The meanings of these bonfires are to burn that which is devilish and impure, leaving only the purity and divinity after Holi. However, we must remember not only to partake in the merry-making of a bonfire. We must remember to sacrifice that within us which is devilish and impure. There is some demon-nature in all of us. We must burn that demon-nature on Holi and emerge as pure and pious as divine Prahlaad.

The fire of purity and divinity which we light on Holi must burn continuously in our hearts throughout the year. We must have an ever-burning bonfire of impurity, so that we are continuously renewed, continuously purified and continuously rejuvenated.

On Holi we sing loudly in Hindi, "Holi I, Holi I, Holi I..."

However, let us not just chant this rhyme; rather, let us truly pray to God that on this day "I" may become holy. Let us pray that "I" may become as pious, pure and devoted as Prahlaad. In that way, our lives and our hearts and our souls will be forever protected, forever sheltered at His holy feet.

As we chant "Holi I, Holi I, Holi I...," let us also pray that our "eye" may become holy, that we may be granted the divine vision by which we behold Him in all whom we see. Let us pray that through our holy eye, we never are led toward anger, greed, lust or jealousy.

Let this Holi be a time when we change
not only the color of our faces,
but the color of our hearts.

Let us not only "play" Holi,
but let us become holy.

Let the only color that
truly penetrates our beings
be the color of God.

For, on the morning after Holi,
the other colors will wash away.

We must let the color of God
be indelible in our eyes, in our ears,
and in our hearts.

The Rituals

Fasting

A fast is:	A fast is not:
About God	About food
A time of reflection	A time of hunger
For peace of the body, mind and spirit	For *pakoras, phalahari chapatis*, and *puris*
A day of discipline	A day of dieting
To purify you	To frustrate you

Today, fasting has become a great trend across the world. In any bookstore you will find volumes of literature extolling one fast or another – juice fasts, water fasts, fruit fasts, and so on. Fasting is frequently heralded as the "miracle weight loss" for those who have tried all else without success.

Connection with the Divine

However, while fasting is certainly of great health benefit, to define it merely as a type of "diet" is to undermine one of the oldest and most sacred spiritual practices. Fasting has been used for millennia by the *rishis*, saints and sages in order to purify their bodies, minds and souls and to bring every cell of their bodies into connection with the Divine.

A True Fast

A true fast, undertaken with understanding and discipline, has the ability to restore all systems of the body. The nervous, circulatory, digestive, respiratory and reproductive systems are all regenerated. The toxins and impurities in our blood and tissues are eliminated and our system becomes rejuvenated. The majority of all today's terminal illnesses are rooted in over-consumption, so a fast purifies our bodies from the excess of not only food but also preservatives, chemicals and toxins.

A fast also is one of the best ways of controlling our mind and senses. Fasts have been used for millennia to subdue passion, anger and lust. They allow us to withdraw our senses from the outside world and become refocused on our own divine nature and our connection to God. Additionally, during this period of *sadhana*, austerity, and restraint one realizes that one is truly the master of one's body, not vice versa.

Unfortunately, many people in the Indian community seem to have forgotten much of the purpose of a fast. Today, you will see people with plates overflowing with *puris* and *pakoras* who say they are fasting. There are *phalahari chapatis, saboodana kichari* and so many other hearty foods that we barely even notice it is a fast. I have heard that there is even a recipe for *phalahari* pizza dough!

On the one hand, it is wonderful to see such a proliferation of the idea of *phalahar* (the taking of foods not made from cereals, such as fruits), and I am glad to see that observing weekly fasts, or fasts on *Ekadashi*, are rituals which have not been lost as we enter the 21ˢᵗ century.

However, it is crucial to pause and reflect on what we are calling a "fast," for although the idea of fasting is still upheld with great fervor, its true meaning and purpose can be obscured by the latest *phalahar* recipes.

Upvas

In Sanskrit, the word for fast is *upvas*. *Upvas* literally means, "sitting near to." Sitting near to whom? Near to God.

Fasting is a time in which our bodies are light, a time in which our vital energy is not being dissipated through the process of consumption and digestion, a time in which we are free from the heaviness and lethargy resulting from over-indulgence.

However, a fast is not meant to be merely a refrain from eating. In fact, it is not necessary to refrain entirely from food on the day of a fast. Fruits and milk enable our bodies to remain strong and active while simultaneously giving us the benefit of a "fast." *Upvas*, however, is not as simple as reducing one's caloric intake or avoiding certain foods. *Upvas* is not a time in which only our stomach is free from excessive external stimulation. It is not a time of mere restraint of the tongue. *Upvas* should be a time in which all of our organs are restrained. It should be a time in which all of our organs are purified, a time in which every sense is turned toward the Divine.

Our tongues should refrain from both indulgence in food and drink, as well as from indulgence in speech. A fast should be a time during which we observe as much silence as possible, for we lose much of our vital energy in speech, and through speech our focus becomes diverted outward.

A Fast For All Senses

We tend to think that we only "eat" through our mouths, that our meals are the only "food" our bodies get. However, what we hear, what we see, what we touch – all these things are taken into our bodies as food. Just as pure, wholesome food brings us health of the body, pure wholesome sights, sounds and other stimuli bring health to the mind, heart and soul. Therefore, when we undertake a fast, we must be equally as aware of purifying the food that we take in through our eyes, ears and hands as we are of the food that we take in through our mouths.

During our fast, our ears should refrain from hearing anything other than chanting of the Lord's name, positive conservation which is peaceful, pious and beneficial, or the quiet of our own thoughts. During a fast we should not listen to music with harsh lyrics, watch TV, or be part of idle gossip. So frequently we see people at temple who have spent the whole day "fasting" who then come to the temple and huddle together, gossiping and chatting. Their bodies may be hungry, but their souls have not fasted.

Additionally, that which we see – frequently without even noticing it – penetrates our minds and hearts and changes our perspective. The simple sight of a woman's bare leg may arouse lust in an otherwise simple and pious man; the sight of blood might cause nausea and panic in one who is usually calm; the sight of a enemy might immediately evoke animosity in one who is usually peaceful and loving.

When we fast we must limit all stimuli which we perceive. That is why we should "sit near to God." Sit at the temple – either the temple in your home or in the actual *mandir*. Or, if you prefer, be with nature. Just make sure that as much as possible the sights and the sounds which you "imbibe" during your fast are pure, pious, loving and filled with divinity. Even if you go to work or to school during your fast, try as much as possible to avoid those situations in which you will see or hear things that are arousing, disturbing or distracting. If there is a way to drive to work or school that may be perhaps a few minutes longer but takes you through a tree-lined road rather than the packed freeway, take the nicer drive. If you can spend your lunch break walking in a park or with your eyes closed in meditation, do that instead of sitting in a cafe with your friends. Remember, a fast is not every day.

A day of fasting should be a special day of purification and rememberance of God. Try to take steps that remind you throughout the day that you are "fasting" all of your senses.

During a fast we should also try to quiet our minds as much as possible. So much of our energy is drained each day in our ceaseless, incessant thought process. Frequently this leads only to more confusion and more questions. Therefore, as we give our bodies a rest from digesting food in our stomachs, as we give our ears a rest from digesting impure thoughts, and as we give our eyes a rest from digesting over-stimulating or sensual sights, let us also give our minds a rest from having to digest our thousands upon thousands of thoughts each day.

Weekly Fasts

Many people fast on a particular day of the week. You will notice, for example, on Monday that many people will say, "This is my fast."

The days of the Indian week are in honor of a particular deity or aspect of the Divine. Monday, Somvar, is the day dedicated to Lord Shiva. Tuesday, Mangalvar, is the day dedicated to Hanumanji. Thursday, Guruvar, is the day dedicated to the Guru. It is said that on these particular days, that aspect of the Divine is in the nearest reach of the devotee. So, for example, devotees of Lord Shiva will observe a fast on Mondays in order to offer their respects to the Lord and to seek His blessings. Seekers who are strongly devoted to their Guru will observe a fast on Thursdays, in order to feel "one" with the Guru and to remember Him throughout the course of the day.

However, sometimes we see that these fasts have become merely ritual; the spiritual aspect has been lost in many cases. People observe fast because they've done it for years, or because their parents did it, or because they were instructed to do so. It is a rare and truly divine devotee who truly remembers, throughout the course of the day, that aspect of the divine for whom they are fasting.

Indian culture and Hindu tradition are meant to bring us into close contact with the Divine. They are meant to open up the infinite, glorious channel between us and God. These rituals were given to help us step out of the mundane world and re-realize our divine connection.

The point of a fast is to be light so we can sit comfortably in meditation. The point is to have our energy turned away from food, away from the mundane world and to the divine. The energy which our body saves on digestion gets channeled toward both physical repair of the body as well as toward vital spiritual *Shakti*. The point of being a little hungry is that it reminds us of why we are fasting.

I heard a beautiful story of a great saint who could cure lepers of their oozing wounds. One day, a very sick man came to the saint and she carefully laid her hands over his gaping wounds, and they each instantaneously healed beneath the touch of her divine hands. However, when she sent him away, she had left one wound untreated. Her devotees questioned her, asking why.

Since she clearly had the ability to cure all the wounds, why would she leave one bleeding? Her answer was beautifully apt. She said, "Because it is that one bleeding wound which will keep him calling out to God."

Our lives are extremely busy and filled with so many small errands, appointments and pleasures that we rarely find the time to remember God. I always say that we tell our loved ones, "Oh, I miss you, I miss you," if they are gone for only a few days. But, do we ever find ourselves, with tears streaming down our faces because we are missing God? Those who do are very rare and very divine. Typically, we tend to remember God when there is adversity. Our child is in the ICU after a car accident and so we start to religiously chant mantras. We find a lump in our wife's breast, and we start going religiously to the temple. We are hoping for a promotion at work and so we perform *yagna*. This is not wrong. It is human nature. We are very busy the rest of the time, and we mostly find ourselves turning to God when we need Him.

So, when our *rishis* and saints urged people to fast, part of the reason was to remember God. As we are hungry, we remember, "Oh, yes, today I am fasting." This remembrance that we are fasting then makes us remember God. Even if we cannot take the day off work to sit in puja or meditation, the constant feeling of mild hunger in our bodies will still keep us connected to the reason for the fast, and thus we will be reminded of God throughout the day.

That doesn't mean we must starve ourselves completely.

Those who are working or going to school or whose health does not permit them to fast should not worry. Take fruit, take nuts, take milk. However, try to take as little as is necessary for you to do your daily tasks. Try to leave enough empty room in your stomach that the emptiness causes you to remember that you are fasting. If we fill our stomachs with *pakoras* and *ladoos* and fried potatoes, are we likely to remember God? Try to eat only those things which are easily digestible and thus preserve the vital energy of the body.

The ideal is to remember God all the time. The ideal is that He should be ever with us, ever such an integral part of our minute-to-minute, moment-to-moment existence that we never feel separate. But, this is rare for people, especially for those who are living in the West (or in West-ernized India) and are constantly inundated with tasks and jobs and propaganda telling them that they must buy more, own more and obtain more. Amidst all this, many, understandably, find it difficult to keep God in the center of their lives. That is the beauty of the fast – even unconsciously, you are reminded every moment that "Today is a special day. Today I am fasting for Hanumanji [or for Lord Shiva, or for my Guru.]"

If we satiate our hunger with platefuls of *phalahar*, then in many ways we have defeated the purpose.

Ekadashi

Twice a month we observe *Ekadashi*. The eleventh day of

each lunar cycle (both lunar fortnights) is observed as a special *Ekadashi* fast. There are many *Ekadashis* during the course of the year, each with a slightly different significance. The importance of observing *Ekadashi* is written in both the *Puranas* as well as in the *Upanishads*. It is said that by observing one *Ekadashi* fast with reverence, devotion, purity and strictness, one attains all of the benefits of performing a wide range of extended austerities.

However, *Ekadashi* is of an importance far greater than simply the restraint from rice and grains. It symbolizes the control of the mind.

Our *Upanishads* say that to control the mind is the greatest task and the greatest accomplishment. They say that when the mind is under control, all else – the senses, the body – will follow. "The body is the chariot, the senses are the horses pulling the chariot, and the mind is the driver with the reigns in his hands." So, if the driver is calm, pious and peaceful, he will drive the horses, and thereby the chariot, toward peace, love and God. But, if the driver is tempestuous and intractable, then the horses jump and buck wildly, leading the chariot to thrash here and there, eventually collapsing upon itself.

Our scriptures say we have ten sense organs, and the mind is the eleventh. *Ekadashi* stands for the eleventh, and since the moon is symbolic of the mind, the eleventh day of the lunar cycle thus becomes especially conducive to practices which teach us control of the mind.

Ekadashi is, therefore, a fast for the control of the mind. It is said that if a seeker observes even one *Ekadashi* with true commitment, faith and devotion and if the seeker keeps his mind entirely focused on God during the course of the *Ekadashi*, this seeker will be free from all *karmic* cycles of birth and death.

The *Puranas* encourage complete fasting on *Ekadashi*, but they allow those who are weak to take roots, fruit, milk and water. This is important, because the scriptures specifically state that this is only for those who are weak. Today, however, we can also extrapolate from that to mean those who would become weak (and therefore unable to perform their tasks) if they abstain completely from all food. There are many students and others whose jobs or studies are so taxing and straining that the body requires some caloric intake. For these people, it is fine to take fruit, juices and milk. But, unless it is necessary, people should refrain as much as possible from eating at all on the *Ekadashi* fast. When it is necessary, fruits and milk should be taken in their purest, simplest, most unadulterated forms.

Further, it is said that the day of *Ekadashi* is meant to be spent chanting the holy names of Vishnu and performing sacred Vishnu *puja*. If we are able to take the day off of work and do this, it is wonderful. If not, we should be sure that at least some time is spent in the morning before leaving home, in meditation on the holy form of Vishnu and chanting His name. If we must be at school or work during the day, let us vow that at least every two or three hours we will take a five minute break and sit silently, chanting God's name. Let us also vow that when we return home at the end of the day we will spend special, extra time in meditation and in prayer. A fasting day should feel more divine and more holy than other days, but it is up to us to make the choices and decisions which will lead to that special feeling.

If we truly want to reap the spiritual and physical benefits of fasting, we must follow the principles laid out by the sages and saints. These principles urge us to refrain from filling any of our senses (mouths, eyes or ears) with that which is unholy, and urge us to spend our "fast" engaged in contemplation of the Divine.

Let us all vow to observe fasts. What exactly you eat or don't eat is not as important as the spirit in which the fast is done. Unless you are performing a very specific fast for a very specific occasion or ritual, the little details are not so important. What is important is that the day of the fast is a day that you are with God. Be light. Be restrained. Be disciplined. Be focused.

Aarti

Aarti is a beautiful ceremony in which *dias* (oil lamps) are offered to God. *Aarti* can be done to a deity in the temple, it can be done on the banks of the Ganges to Mother Ganga, or it can be done to a saint. It is performed to God, in any manifestation, any form, by any name.

In the *Aarti* ceremony, the devotee waves the oil lamp burning with ghee and camphor from the eye to the feet, back to the eye and back to the feet of the Divine. Typically, this is performed three times.

The essence of the *Aarti* ceremony is that all day long God offers us light – the light of the sun, the light of life, the light of His (Her) blessings. *Aarti* is a time when we say "thank you," and we offer back the light of our thanks, the light of our love and the light of our devotion.

We realize that the small *deepa* is nothing compared to the divine light which shines on us all day. So, *Aarti* is a ceremony of humility, a time in which we acknowledge that "God, you are everything. I am nothing. All day you shine upon the world. All I can offer you is this small *deepa*, a flame which will be blown out by the passing wind. But, I offer it with devotion and with love. Please accept my offering."

One of the meanings of *Aarti* literally is "remover of pain."
This is beautiful, because there is nothing inherent in the
name of the ceremony that says which form or name of
God it should be performed to. It should be performed
to the Divine Remover of Pain in our life.

Yagna/Havan

The meanings of *yagna* are vast and varied, enough to fill a book by themselves. *Yagna* can refer literally to the *havan*/fire ceremony, where we sit around a fire, placing offerings into the flames. It can also be used to mean *seva* or "sacrifice." The most common usage, though, is the *yagna* which refers to the *havan* ceremony, involving a large fire. It is this meaning of *yagna* that I will elucidate here.

The *havan* is one of the most common rituals in Indian culture. It is used on most important occasions, ranging from weddings to the opening of new businesses to graduations to prayers for someone's health.

The offering which is placed into the fire consists of several elements, including *jav*, sesame seeds, rice, ghee, incense and sandalwood. Each element has a different significance. It is said that inhaling the smoke of a holy *yagna* fire has the ability to cure ailments of the lungs or respiratory system.

Havan is, in essence, a purifying ritual. Just as fire purifies everything it touches, so we perform *yagna* that we may be made pure. But who is the Divine Purifier, the True Purifier, the Fire of all fires? God. So, these offerings are not being made simply to a fire, rather they are being made to the Real Fire, the Almighty. As we place the *ahuti* (offerings) into the flames, we symbolically offer all our "impurities" – our anger, our greed, our jealousy, our grudges, our pains, our obstacles – and we pray to God to make us as pure as the ghee we are pouring into the flames.

Also, the *yagna* reminds us to give and give and give. One of the key aspects of a *yagna* is the mantra. The mantras are special, sacred mantras which beseech God to accept our offering and to bless us. The mantras go on and on and with each mantra we place an offering into the flames. This is to teach us that our hands should never be empty of offerings. We should continually give and give, with every breath. At the end of each mantra and *shloka* chanted by the priests, it says, "*Idam namamah, idam namamah.*" This means, "Not for me, but for You." It reminds us that everything we do in life must be for others, for God, for the world, rather than for our own selfish motives. This is the root of *yagna*, the root of Hinduism and the root of happiness in life.

The *ahuti* (offering) is made up of a variety of seeds. These seeds symbolize our ego. Just as a seed planted in rich, fertile soil will flower, blossom and grow its roots into the ground, so will our egos grow and strengthen if we nurture and nourish them. Yet, a seed that has been roasted can never germinate. So, we offer our egos to God – to the divine Fire – and pray that He will burn our egos in the fire of His grace.

We sit around the *yagna* to remind us to keep God and purity in the center of our lives. Too often, we want to be the center of everything; we want to be the most important; we want offerings to be made to us. That is the root of our unhappiness. So, in a *yagna*, we sit around the fire and place our offerings inward. This reminds us that in life we should be on the outside, with God in the center, and we should just offer in, offer in – offering our every breath, every thought, every action at His holy feet, praying for Him to purify us.

Lastly, just as the flames of a fire only rise higher and higher, so we pray that God may carry our lives only upward, closer and closer to His divine abode.

Prana Pratishtha Ceremony

A Hindu Temple is a sacred place, endowed with divine energies and powers. At the heart of each temple lie the deities, to whom we bow and pray in worship. Why is it though that these statues, these "idols," are worshipped as God? How did they come to be infused with divine characteristics? The answer is the *Prana Pratishtha* ceremony. The *Prana Pratishtha* ceremony is the time in which the Divine *Prana*, the Divine Life Force, is infused into the *murtis*, making them true embodiments of the Divine Energy.

People say that Hindus are idol worshippers. We are not. We are ideal worshippers. It is not the plaster and marble and stone we revere; rather it is the presence of God which has been transmitted into these otherwise lifeless statues. The rites and rituals of *Prana Pratishtha* are followed strictly according to the Agamic texts. Prior to installation, priests who have been well-trained in Vedic rituals perform specific mantras and *pujas* which have been shown to endow an inanimate object with divine life and energy.

These mantras and rites begin with the simple man who sculpts the stone. He is not an ordinary artist. Rather, he is one who has been blessed with the ability to create a physical manifestation of God. He performs *puja* and prayer prior to and during the sculpting. He maintains, in his mind, the vision of the deity he is sculpting. He prays for God to come to life in his statue. His work area looks more like a temple than an art studio. So, from the very first moment, the stone is treated with reverence and piety, preparing it to carry the force of God.

Then, when the *murtis* are finished and taken to the temple, the special *Prana Pratishtha* ceremony takes place, typically lasting for five days. During this time, numerous special rites and rituals are performed and mantras are chanted. It is after this complex set of sacred rituals that the *murtis* become infused with divine power and truly embody the God in whose manifest form they are created. The final *puja* is performed on a special, auspicious day according to the lunar calendar, when the sun is without spots. On that day, the eyes of the deity are opened, giving them the divine ability to give *darshan* to devotees. The eyes are opened either by the sculptor himself, or by a revered holy saint or priest.

At this point, they are no longer *murtis*. They are deities. After this, we no longer refer to the stone or other materials of which they are constructed. For, they have become sanctified and are now only a physical manifestation of aspects of the Supreme Godhead. They are no longer marble. They are now divine. "Whatever form of Me any devotee worships with faith, I come alive in that form," says the *Bhagavad Gita*.

Once the *Prana Pratishtha* ceremony has been performed, the deity must be worshipped in a special way at least twice a day. Additionally, a deity whose *Prana Pratishtha* ceremony has been performed cannot be moved. For that reason – and for the numerous specific rituals which must be performed after the *Prana Pratishtha* ceremony on a daily basis – it is not recommended to have *Prana Pratishtha* ceremonies for deities in a home.

Some people may ask why we need deities, if God exists everywhere. It is very difficult for most people to envision the unmanifest, ever-present, all-pervading Supreme Being. It is easier for us to focus our attention and our love on an image of Him. It is easier to display love, affection and devotion to a physical deity than to a transcendent, omnipresent existence. Additionally, through the *Prana Pratishtha* ceremony and through our own faith and piety, this image of Him truly comes alive and become Him. So, by worshipping His image with faith and love, we arrive at His holy feet.

In the *Srimad Bhagavatum*, Lord Krishna says, "Whenever one develops faith in Me – in My manifest form as the Deity or in any other of my manifestations – one should worship Me in that form. I exist within all created beings as well as separately in both My unmanifest and manifest forms. I am the Supreme Soul of all."

ABOUT THE AUTHOR

His Holiness Pujya Swami Chidanand Saraswatiji

Spiritual and Academic Education: H.H. Swami Chidanand Saraswatiji's motto in life is, "In the Service of God and humanity." Touched by the hand of God at the tender age of eight, Pujya Swamiji left His home to live a life devoted to God and humanity, spending His youth in silence, meditation and austerities high in the Himalayas. At the age of seventeen, after nine years of unbroken, intense *sadhana*, He returned from the forest—under the orders of His guru—and obtained an academic education to parallel His spiritual one. Pujya Swamiji has master's degrees in Sanskrit and Philosophy as well as fluency in many languages.

The Teaching of Unity: Unity, harmony, and the belief in infinite paths to God are the foundation of Pujya Swamiji's "religion." His goal is to bring everyone closer to God, regardless of what name one uses. "If you are a Hindu, be a better Hindu. If you are a Christian, be a better Christian. If you are a Muslim, be a better Muslim. If you are a Jew, be a better Jew," He says.

In this line, He has been a leader in numerous international, inter-faith conferences and parliaments, including the **Parliament of World Religions**; the **Millennium World Peace Summit of Religious and Spiritual Leaders at the United Nations**; the **World Economic Forum**; the **World Council of Religious Leaders at the United Nations**; the **World Conference of Religions for Peace**; the **Global Youth Peace Summit at the United Nations**; the **Hindu-Jewish Summit**; and the **Hindu-Christian Dialogue initiated by the Vatican**. He is also a leader of frequent pilgrimages for peace across the world.

Spiritual Leader and Inspiration: Pujya Swamiji is the President and Spiritual Head of Parmarth Niketan Ashram in Rishikesh, one of India's largest and most renowned spiritual institutions. Under His divine inspiration and leadership, Parmarth Niketan has become a sanctuary known across the globe as one filled with grace, beauty, serenity and true divine bliss. Pujya Swamiji has also increased several-fold the humanitarian activities undertaken by Parmarth Niketan. Now, the ashram is not only a spiritual haven for those who visit, but it also provides education, training, and health care to those in need.

He is also the founder and the spiritual head of the first Hindu-Jain Temple in America. This beautiful, three-domed masterpiece is located on the outskirts of Pittsburgh, Pennsylvania, and has paved the way for unity between Hindus and Jains across America. Pujya Swamiji is also the founder and inspiration behind many other temples in the USA, Canada, Europe and Australia.

Guide to Youth: Pujya Swamiji knows that the youth are our future, and He is forever changing the course of that future through His profound effect on every youngster with whom He comes in contact. Children and adolescents seem to bloom like flowers under the rays of His light. Additionally, He gives pragmatic tools to help them unite in the spirit of peace, harmony and global change. Pujya Swamiji runs youth sessions and camps in the USA, Europe and throughout Asia.

Ceaseless Service: "Giving is Living" is Pujya Swamiji's motto; He is always in the midst of dozens of projects, each one a noble and tenaciously dedicated effort to make the world a better place for all of humanity. He is the Founder/Chairman of the India Heritage Research Foundation (IHRF), an international, non-profit, humanitarian organization dedicated to providing education, health care, youth welfare, and vocational training to the needy population. IHRF also, under the guidance and inspiration of Pujya Swamiji, is compiling the first *Encyclopedia of Hinduism* in history. Pujya Swamiji is also the Founder/

Chairman of the Divine Shakti Foundation, a non-profit organization dedicated to using the energy, strength and capability of women to help bring the light of life, hope, education and assistance to the abandoned, orphaned babies and young girls, as well as widowed and impoverished women.

Ganga Action: Pujya Swamiji is also the Founder of Ganga Action Parivar (GAP), a worldwide family of scientists, engineers, specialists, volunteers and devotees who are dedicated to working to make Mother Ganga's waters not only *nirmal* (clean) but also *aviral* (free-flowing). The work being undertaken by GAP is multi-faceted and extensive. See the separate GAP section and also www.gangaaction.com for more details.

Awards and Recognitions: Pujya Swamiji is the recipient of innumerable awards for both His role as spiritual leader as well as for His unparalleled humanitarian work. Some of the more noteworthy are as follows:

1. Mahatma Gandhi Humanitarian Award, given by the Mayor of New Jersey, USA for outstanding charitable and interfaith work

2. Hindu of the Year, 1991,by the international magazine *Hinduism Today*, for masterminding the project of the next millennium, the *Encyclopedia of Hinduism*

3. Uttaranchal Ratan ("Jewel of the State of Uttaranchal") Award

4. Bharat Vikas Parishad 1st Utkrishtta Samman Award

5. Devarishi Award, by Sandipani Vidya Niketan, under the guidance of Pujya Sant Rameshbhai Oza, for promoting Indian culture and heritage across the world

6. Bhaskar Award, 1998, by Mystic India and Bharat Nirman,

for Outstanding Humanitarian Service

7. Prominent Personality Award, by Lions' Club

8. Diwaliben Mohanlal Mehta Charitable Trust Award for Progress in Religion

9. Best Citizens of India Award

Further, He has been given the title of Patron of the Russian Indian Heritage Research Foundation, Moscow, and is also a Patron of the Centre for Religious Experience in Oxford, UK.

The True *Sanyasi*: Pujya Swamiji seems unaffected by this incredible list of accomplishments and remains a pious child of God, owning nothing, draped in saffron robes, living a life of true renunciation. His days in Rishikesh are spent offering service to those around Him. Thousands travel from America, Europe and Australia as well as from all over India, simply to sit in His presence and receive His *darshan*. To them, the journey is an inconsequential price to pay for the priceless gift of His *satsang*. He travels the world, bringing the light of wisdom, inspiration, upliftment and the divine touch to thousands across the world.

INDIA HERITAGE RESEARCH FOUNDATION

Pujya Swami Chidanand Saraswatiji is the founder and chairman of the India Heritage Research Foundation, a non-profit, charitable organization dedicated to humanitarian and cultural projects. Founded in 1987, IHRF is committed to preserving the timeless wisdom and ageless grandeur of Indian culture. By weaving together ancient tradition, cultural history, a wide range of non-discriminatory charitable services, and inspiring youth programs, IHRF has created a tapestry of true, universal beauty.

The Encyclopedia of Hinduism

IHRF has completed the revolutionary project of compiling the first *Encyclopedia of Hinduism* in history. The *Encyclopedia* will mark the first time that the urgent need is met for an authentic, objective and insightful well of information, capturing both the staples and the spices of Indian tradition and culture. This eleven-volume work was previewed and blessed by the hands of the Dalai Lama and many other revered saints at a large function during the Maha Kumbha Mela in Haridwar in 2010, and will be available internationally by the end of 2011.

The *Encyclopedia of Hinduism* will be a significant landmark, encompassing the entire spectrum of the land called Bharat.

IHRF is dedicated to youth, education, spirituality, culture, inter-faith harmony, health care and ecology. To this end, it sponsors medical care programs, schools, *gurukuls*/orphanages, training centers, large-scale spiritual and cultural events, tree-plantation and clean-up programs, conferences geared toward inter-faith harmony, summer camps, and international youth awareness programs. Additionally, IHRF sponsors (both financially and otherwise) educational institutions that are already established but suffering from lack of resources.

Following are examples of only a few of the numerous ways that IHRF's arms embrace humanity:

Y.E.S. – Youth Education Services

Many villages throughout India are oceans of poverty and illiteracy. The influx of technology, commerce, education and metropolitanism that  has flooded most of India's cities since independence seems to have not even touched these villages. They exist as they did centuries ago. However, one crucial change has occurred. Now, basic education and marketable skills are absolute necessities in order to subsist in even the smallest communities. Hence, those who lack this education and training go to sleep hungry each night.

In the midst of this ocean of destitution, there are islands of light, islands of knowledge, islands of hope. The Y.E.S. schools are some of these islands. The Y.E.S. program encompasses dozens of children's schools, women's vocational training programs (including sewing, handicrafts, tailoring and fashion designing as well as adult literacy education), and two orphanages/*gurukuls*. These schools are located in Rishikesh, Swargashram, Rani Pokhri, Lucknow, Himachal Pradesh, Orissa, Uttarkashi, as well as other areas of the Himalayas and North-East India.

The children and women in the Y.E.S. program are given not only an education, but they are also given the priceless gifts of hope and faith.

The Y.E.S. program is dedicated to providing poor and orphaned children a positive, nurturing environment, and to giving them the chance to live a life free from destitution or despair.

Gurukuls/Orphanages

One visit to India is sufficient to see the urgent, dire need for orphanages

and homes for underprivileged children. However, simple shelters with food, beds and babysitters are not sufficient.

These children need not only to be fed and sheltered. Rather, they also need to be educated and trained so they can become productive members of society. They need to be inculcated with values, ethics and spirituality which will make them torchbearers of Indian culture.

Our three *Gurukuls*/Orphanages serve as places where nearly 500 children are housed as well as educated, cultured and filled with crucial values such as non-violence, truth, and *seva*.

Their days are filled with academic and computer studies, *yoga*, meditation, Vedic chanting, reading of scriptures, *seva* and special programs, such as the performance of dramas based on Indian spiritual history, designed to instill in them essential *sanskaras*. Renamed *rishikumars*, the children travel on *yatra* to the Himalayas and perform *yagna* and prayers every night on the banks of Mother Ganga.

Looks of hopelessness have become looks of optimism and hope. Lightless eyes have become bright, shining eyes. Feelings of destitution and despair have become feelings of pride, faith and enthusiasm.

Mansarover Ashrams and Clinic

Under the guidance, inspiration and vision of Pujya Swami Chidanand Saraswatiji, IHRF has built three ashrams and a medical clinic in the holy land of Lake Mansarovar and Mt. Kailash in Tibet.

Prior to this project, there were no indoor lodging facilities nor medical facilities for hundreds of kilometers. People frequently suffered from basic, treatable ailments due to lack of medical attention. Therefore, after undertaking a *yatra* to the sacred land in 1998, Pujya Swamiji took a vow that – by the grace of God – He would do something for the local people (who don't even have running water) and for all the pilgrims who travel there.

The ashram (tourist rest house) and clinic on the banks of Lake Mansarovar were officially inaugurated in July 2003. We have also built two halls there where *satsang*, meditation and many other divine activities can take place.

Additionally, we have built an ashram in Paryang, Tibet, on the way to Mansarovar, the place where every yatri stays one day prior to reaching Mansarovar. This ashram was inaugurated in June 2006.

A third ashram has been built in Dirapuk, on the sacred Mt. Kailash *Parikrama* route, at the unprecedented altitude of 17,000 feet, and

was inaugurated in September 2009. Dirapuk is the place where all pilgrims spend the first night of the two-night, fifty-two kilometer, treacherous *parikrama*. At this location, the *darshan* of Mt. Kailash is the clearest, closest, and most spectacular.

Additionally, we have pledged our support and assistance to the local villagers of Mansarovar.

The project is truly the grace of God and is a divine gift to this holy land, to all Tibetans who live there, and to all the pious pilgrims who cross oceans and continents in order to have a glimpse of the abode of Lord Shiva.

Tsunami Relief

On the 30th of December, 2004, Pujya Swamiji, Vivek Oberoi, Sadhvi Bhagwati, *Rishikumars* from Parmarth Niketan's *Gurukul* and Vivek Oberoi's family traveled down to South India in the wake of the devastating tsunami. Upon seeing the devastation wrought upon the land, they decided to stay and offer both short-term and long-term assistance. The relief work ranged from immediate, emergency measures to the permanent reconstruction of entire villages.

Phase I – Immediate, Emergency Relief Measures

1. Construction of 100 new, temporary homes

2. Establishment and running of seven community kitchens where thousands of families received fresh, hot meals, including milk for children

3. Medical Relief Centers operated at each of the kitchens
4. Playground for the children
5. Free Eye and Cataract Operation Camp for hundreds of villagers

6. Wide-scale distribution of necessities to thousands of people, including food, water, clothing, cooking supplies, shoes, and sheets
7. Repair of over 100 boats and purchase of 15 new boats
8. Purchase of over 600 new fishing nets

Phase II – Permanent Village Reconstruction in Pondicherry

Project Hope undertook the reconstruction of villages Pannithittu and Pattincheri in Pondicherry, totalling over 350 homes. Pannithittu, built through the generosity of Rotary International, Sadeh Lok, UK, Himjyoti Foundation and many other generous donors, was inaugurated in December 2005 by the hands of the Honorable Governors of Tamil Nadu, Pondicherry and Uttarakhand.

The village of Pattincheri, sponsored by Shri LN Mittal of London, was inaugurated in April 2007.

Phase III – Cuddalore Town, Cuddalore District, Tamil Nadu: Orphanage and Women's Center

The final stage in the work was completed and inaugurated on May 12, 2007. The orphanage which we built for the tsunami orphans as well as facilities for over 300 children who had been orphaned prior to the tsunami was inaugurated by H.E. the Honorable Governor of Tamil Nadu, Shri Surjit Singh Barnalaji with Pujya Swamiji.

The orphanage includes dormitory facilities, school rooms, a computer center, medical room, beautiful kitchen and dining facilities, a vocational training center and more. It has been built on the same land as the previously existing home for approximately 200 widowed/abandoned women, which we also beautified. In this way, the orphaned children

will receive, in addition to the staff, mothers, aunts, grandmothers and older sisters; the women will receive the priceless gift of caring for orphaned children. We have also built a vocational training center for the women, and the new huge dining/kitchen facilities are shared by both the children and the women.

Rural Development Program

We are running a rural development program in a town called Veerpur, on the banks of the Ganges, three kilometers south of Rishikesh.

The following are components of the rural development program:

Water facilities – Although the town lies on the banks of the Ganga River, most people had no running water or water for their farms. We dug a boring well and have brought running water to this village.

Tree plantation program

Construction of a proper road in the village

Organic Gardening program – We have started a special organic farming program as well. We have brought in trained organic farmers and scientists to teach the local farmers alternative, chemical-free methods of farming. Further, we will have a special "buy back" program with them where we will buy back from them all of their crops. In addition, the ashram at

Veerpur has its own organic farm.

Women's Vocational training program

Sewage Control and Sanitation programs – We have laid sewage lines in the village and constructed toilets for the villagers so that no pollution goes into Ganga.

Spirituality and Culture – We have started an evening devotional ceremony there on the banks of the Ganges, called *Aarti*. It is a way for the villagers to come together in a spirit of peace, culture & piety.

***Gurukul*/orphanage** – The second of the three *gurukuls*/orphanages is here in Veerpur, and we have plans to open an orphanage for girls here as well.

Project Give Back

With the motto *"Give Back, Feel Good,"* Project Give Back is working to bring medical, environmental and engineering *seva* to the people of rural India by experts and professionals from around the globe. So far, we have been active in organizing and running various free medical camps in the villages of the Himalayas themselves, bringing medical care to the people. Doctors from all over the world of all different specialities come to beautifully donate their skills and expertise to the patients, who usually cannot afford such care, as well as distribute free medicines, glasses and other medical equipment to the patients.

There is also an effort to better educate people to maintain health and

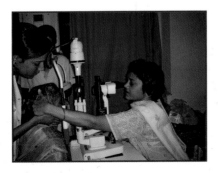

hygiene. We are also working on the establishment of a model village in Veerpur which can serve as a model of environmental preservation and integrity, and which we will then expand into other rural areas.

IHRF is dedicated to bringing food to the hungry, medicine to the sick, and peace to the troubled.

IHRF does not discriminate on the basis of race, religion, caste, gender or nationality.

All of its services are open to all & free to all.

GANGA ACTION PARIVAR

Ganga Action Parivar (GAP) is a world family dedicated to serving Mother Ganga. GAP intends to restore, protect and maintain the River Ganga and Her tributaries in their *aviral* (free-flowing) and *nirmal* (unpolluted) states. Under Pujya Swamiji's guidance and leadership, numerous organizations, scientists, environmentalists, activists, government officials and volunteers are coming together to bring this noble goal to fruition.

GAP was first launched on April 4th, 2010 at a special "Sparsh Ganga" event at Parmarth Niketan Ashram by the hands of Pujya Swamiji, H.H. the Dalai Lama and many revered saints. The event raised awareness about the  need for collective and holistic, solution-based action to address the crucial issues facing the holy river. Many were present to show their support and share their love and dedication towards our environment, and the massive event included participants pledging to help protect and restore the Ganga.

 A similar event was held several weeks later in Gangotri, the source of the river Ganga, with Shri L.K. Advaniji and the Hon'ble Chief Minister of Uttarakhand Ramesh Pokhriyal in which thousands more took pledges to help clean and protect Ganga also.

Under Pujya Swamiji's guidance and leadership, numerous organizations, scientists, environmentalists, activists, government officials and volunteers are coming together to bring this noble goal to fruition. Several conferences have been held to bring these different groups

together. On October 27th, 2010, an Aviral Nirmal Ganga Conference was held at Parmarth Niketan Ashram where prominent spiritual leaders, scientists and experts came to discuss the next steps for addressing the issues facing Ganga, and it was in this conference that the official name "Ganga Action Parivar" was created.

On April 23-24th, 2011, the National Aviral Nirmal Ganga Conference was held at Parmarth Niketan Ashram once again. During this conference, scientists, environmentalists, activistis, government officals and many more came together to find sustainable, implementable solutions for the various issues facing Ganga and her tributaries. The conference was graced by many who are prominent in the movement to clean Ganga, including Shri R.K. Pachauriji, a leading environmental activist who won the Nobel Prize for his work.

Activities of GAP range from working to create sustainable, environmentally-friendly solutions for the various, complex problems facing Ganga and implementing such problems, to holding local clean-ups along Her banks, to educating people about the important and urgent need to live green. *(To learn more, please see www.gangaaction.com.)*

Parmarth Niketan Ashram
Rishikesh (Himalayas), India

H.H. Swami Chidanand Saraswatiji is the President of Parmarth Niketan Ashram in Rishikesh, India, a true, spiritual haven, lying on the holy banks of Mother Ganga, in the lap of the lush Himalayas.

Parmarth Niketan is the largest ashram in Rishikesh. Parmarth Niketan provides its thousands of pilgrims – who come from all corners of the Earth – with a clean, pure and sacred atmosphere as well as abundant, beautiful gardens. With over 1,000 rooms, the facilities are a perfect blend of modern amenities and traditional, spiritual simplicity.

The daily activities at Parmarth Niketan include morning universal prayers, daily *yoga* and meditation classes, daily *satsang* and lecture programs, *kirtan*, world renowned Ganga *aarti* at sunset, as well as

full Nature Cure, and Ayurvedic treatment available on the premises.

Additionally, there are frequently special cultural and spiritual programs given by visiting revered saints, acclaimed musicians, spiritual and social leaders and others.

Further, there are frequent camps in which pilgrims come from across the world to partake in intensive courses on *yoga*, meditation, *pranayama*, stress management, acupressure, Reiki and other ancient Indian sciences. Parmarth Niketan hosts the annual International Yoga Festival from the 1ˢᵗ-7ᵗʰ of March every year, in cooperation with the Government of Uttarakhand.

Parmarth Niketan's charitable activities and services make no distinctions on the basis of caste, color, gender, creed or nationality. Instead they emphasize unity, harmony, peace, global integrity, health, and the holistic connection between the body, mind and spirit.

True to its name, Parmarth Niketan is dedicated to the welfare of all. Everything is open and free to all.